Baubles

Angie's Patterns - Volume 4

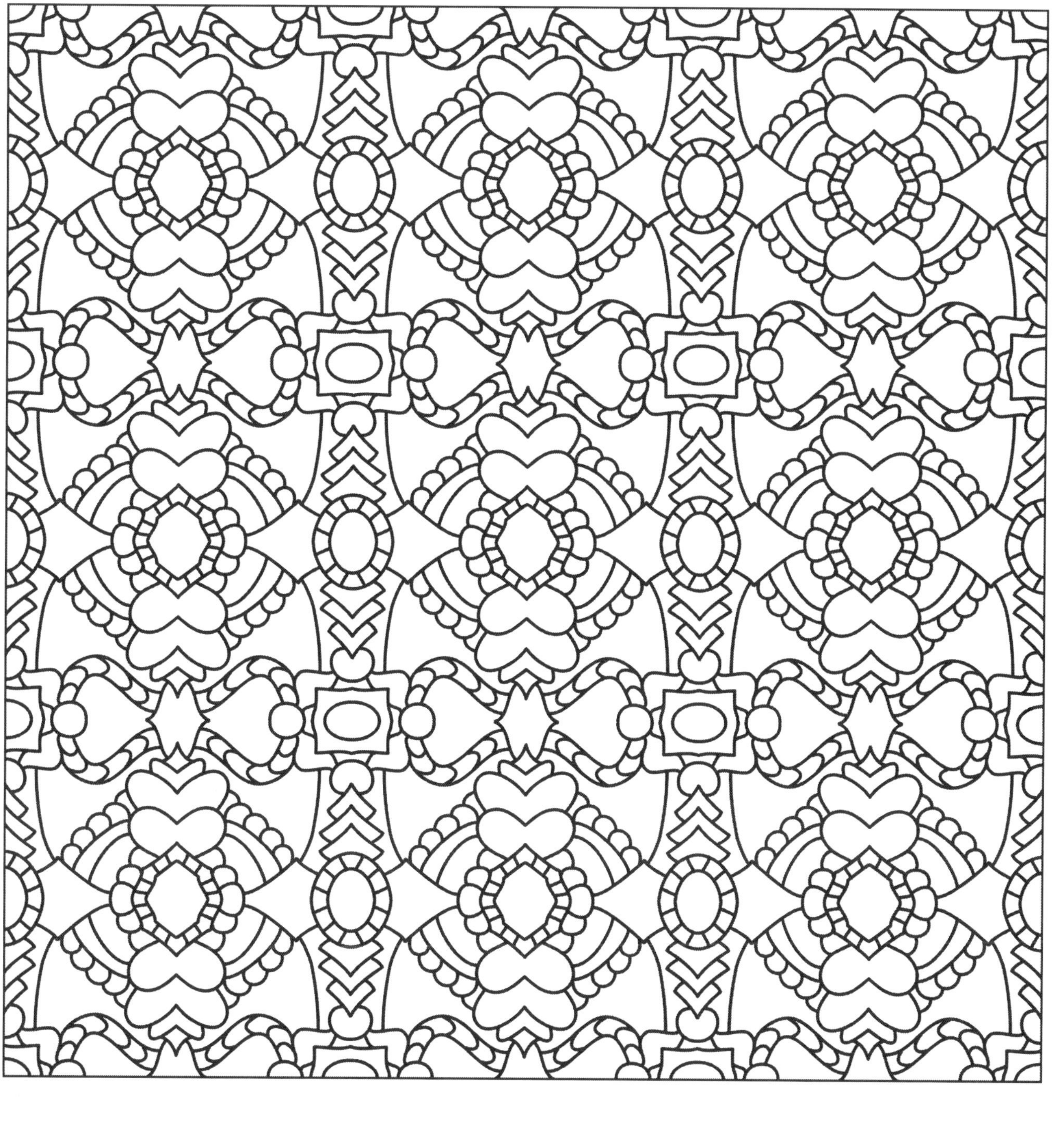

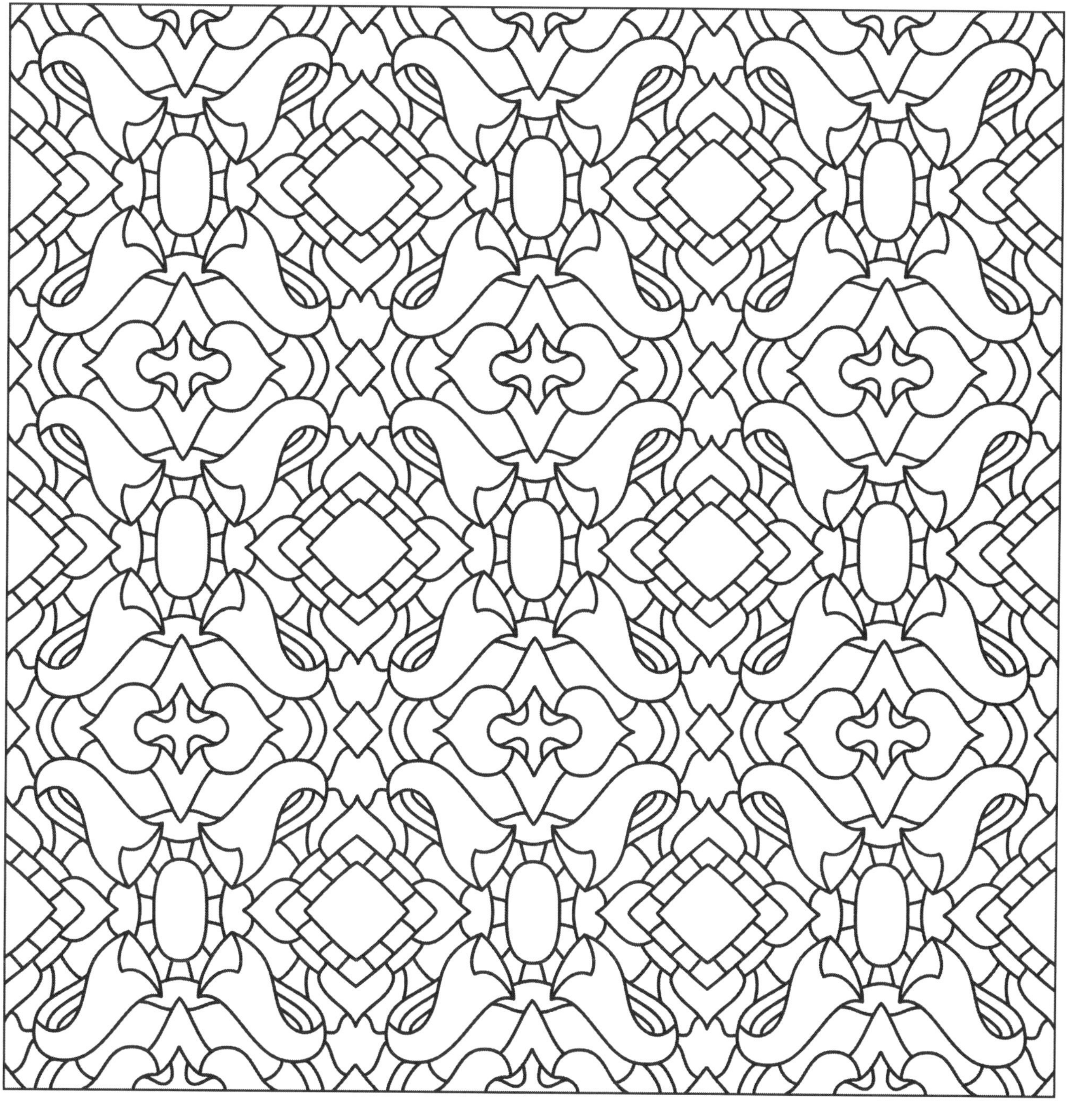

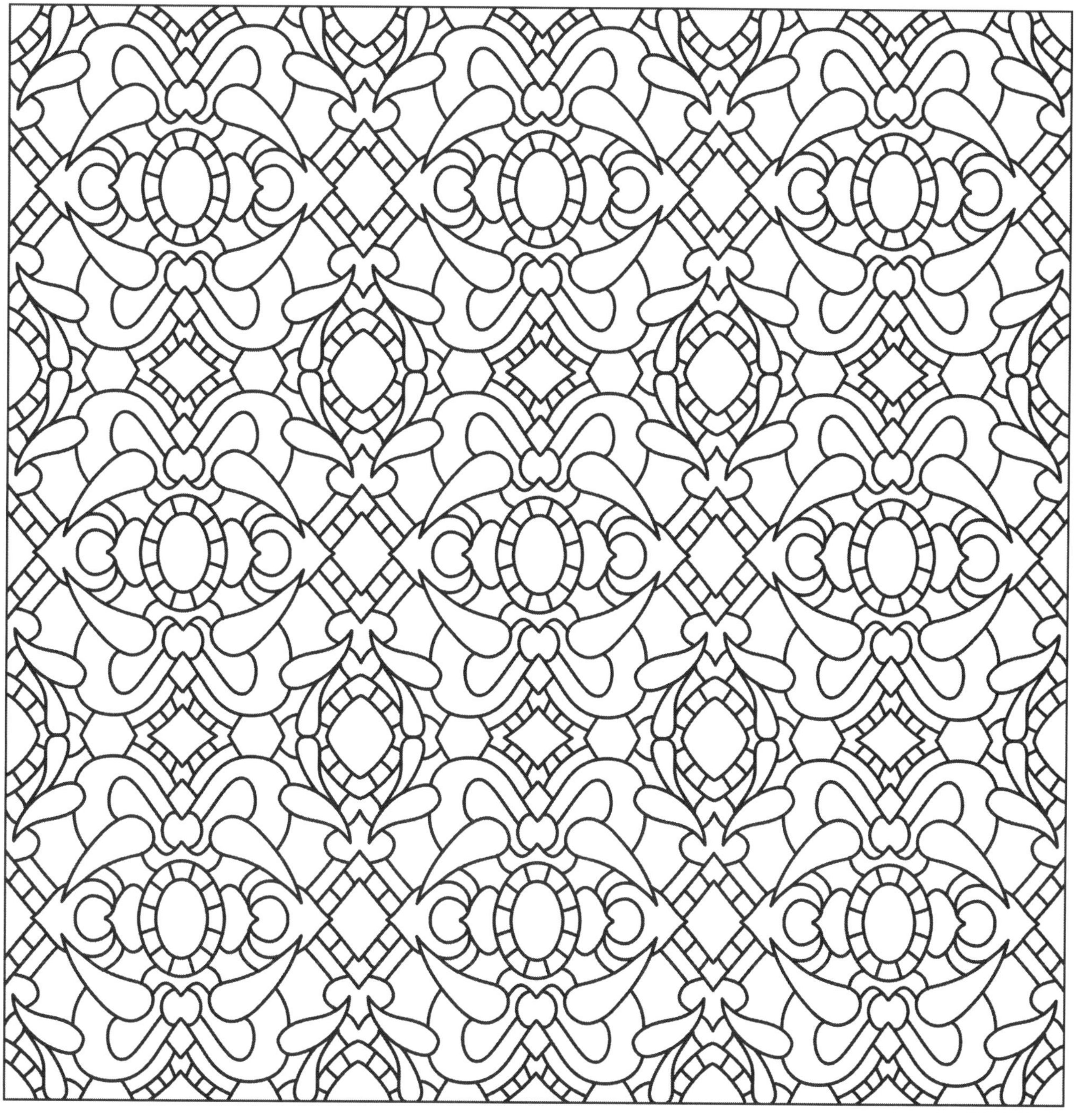

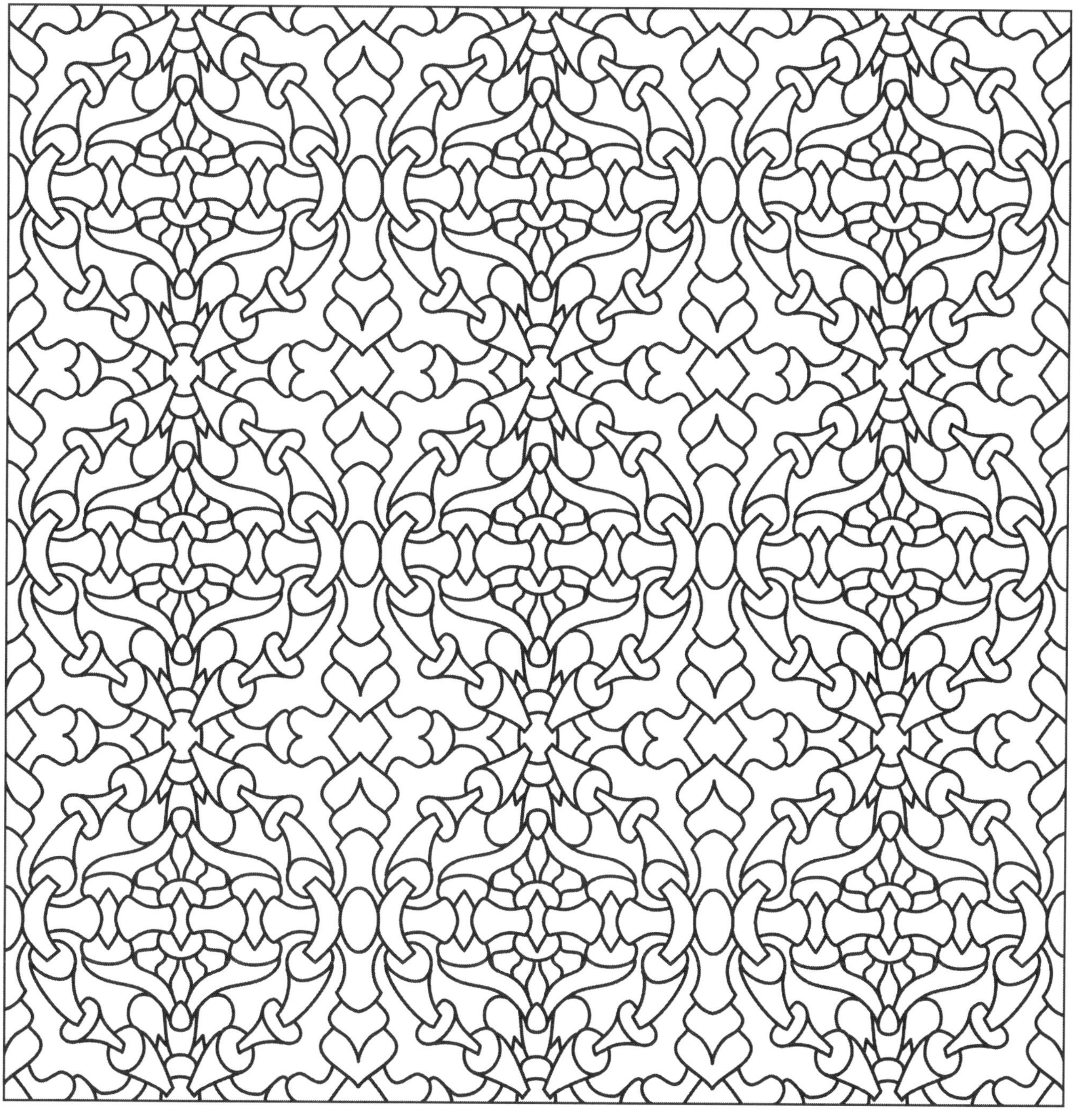

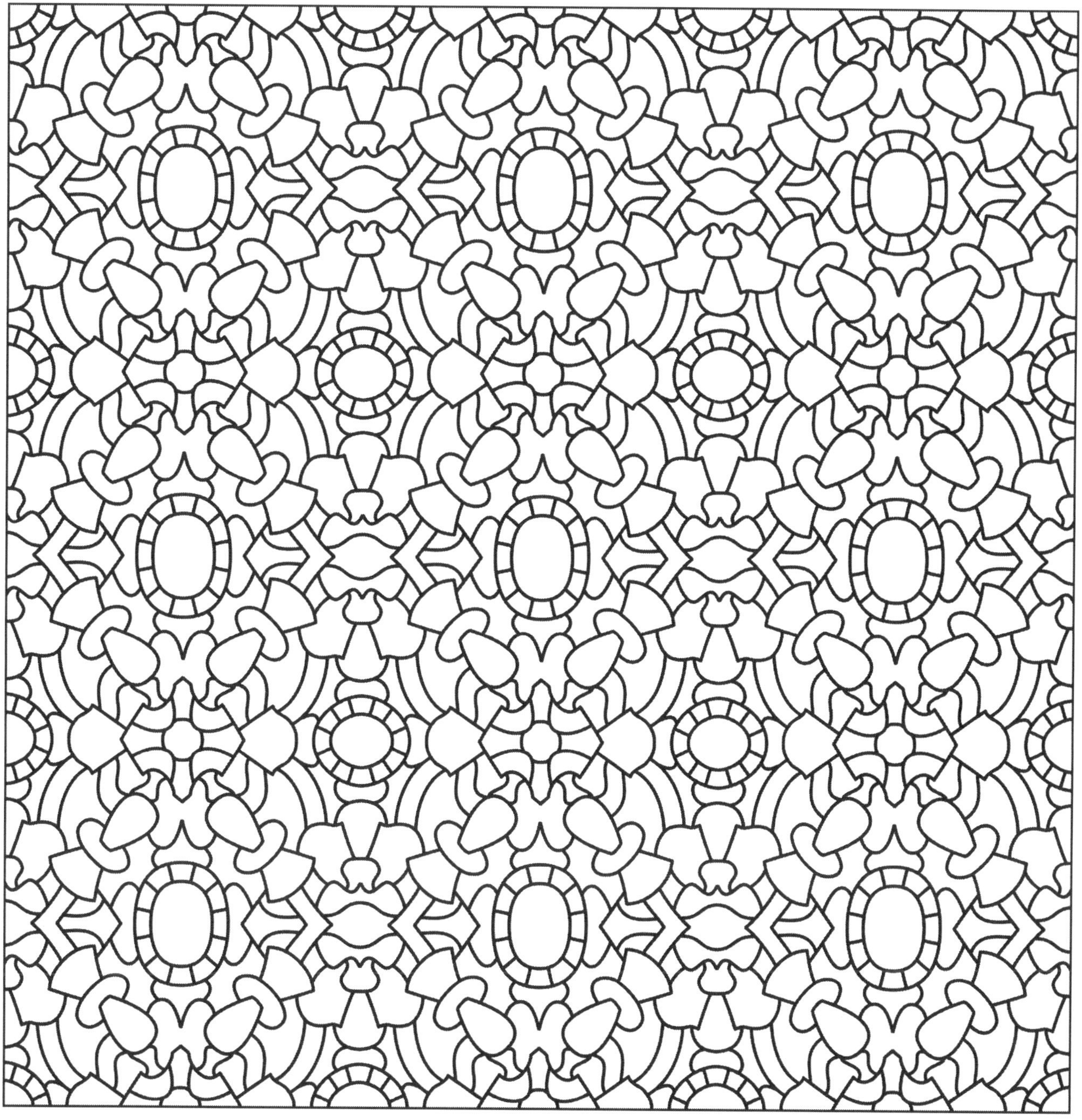

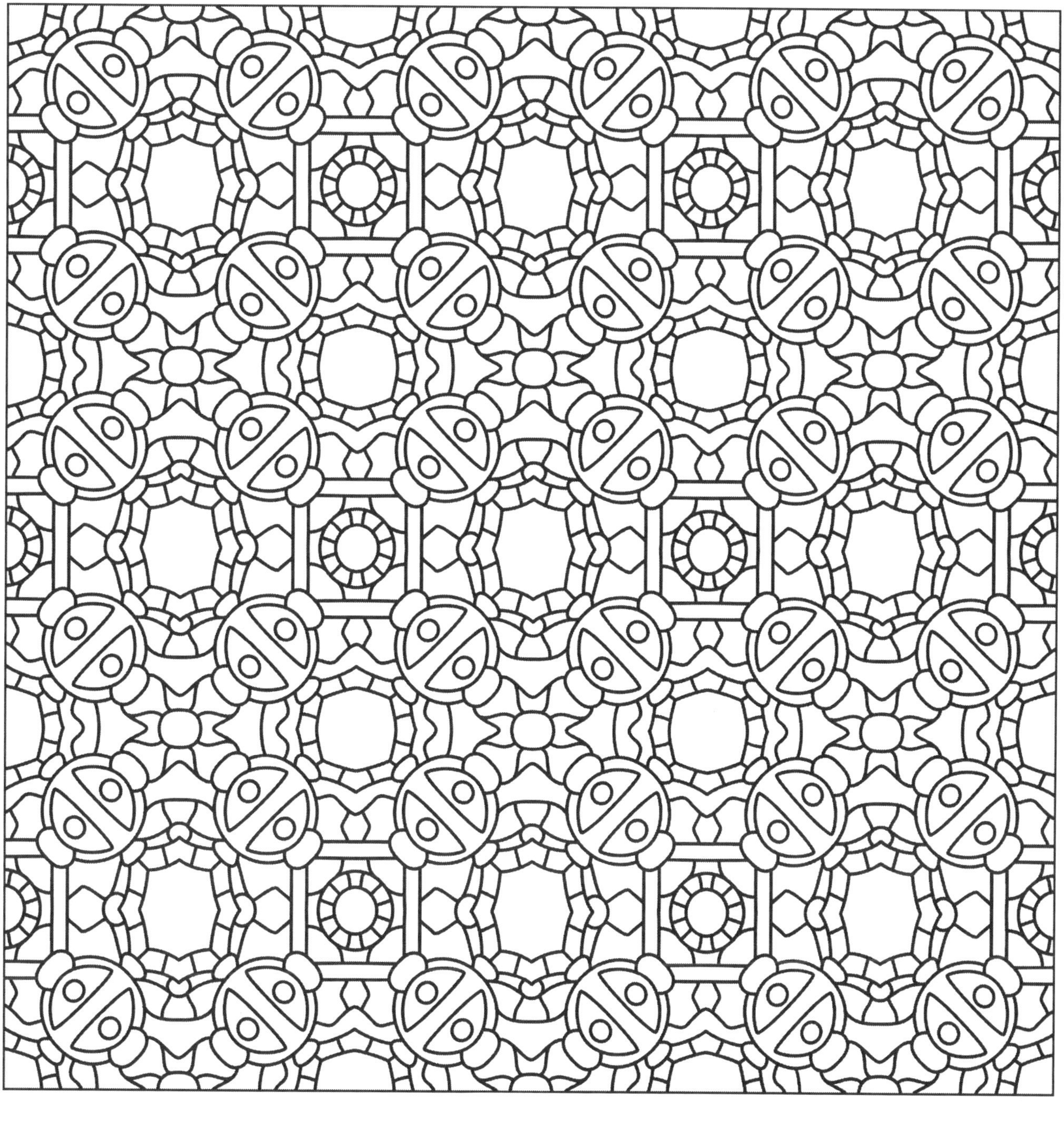

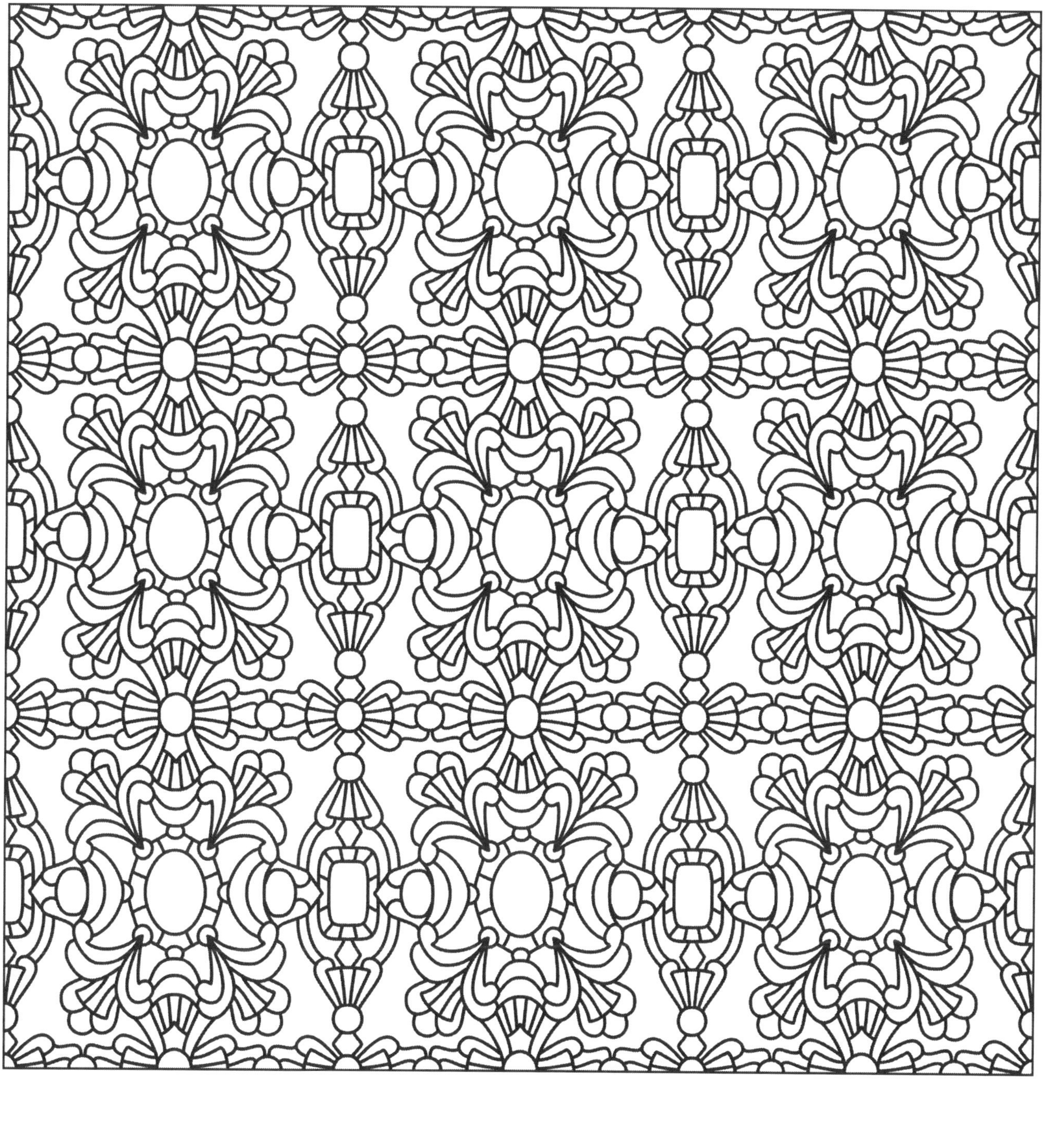

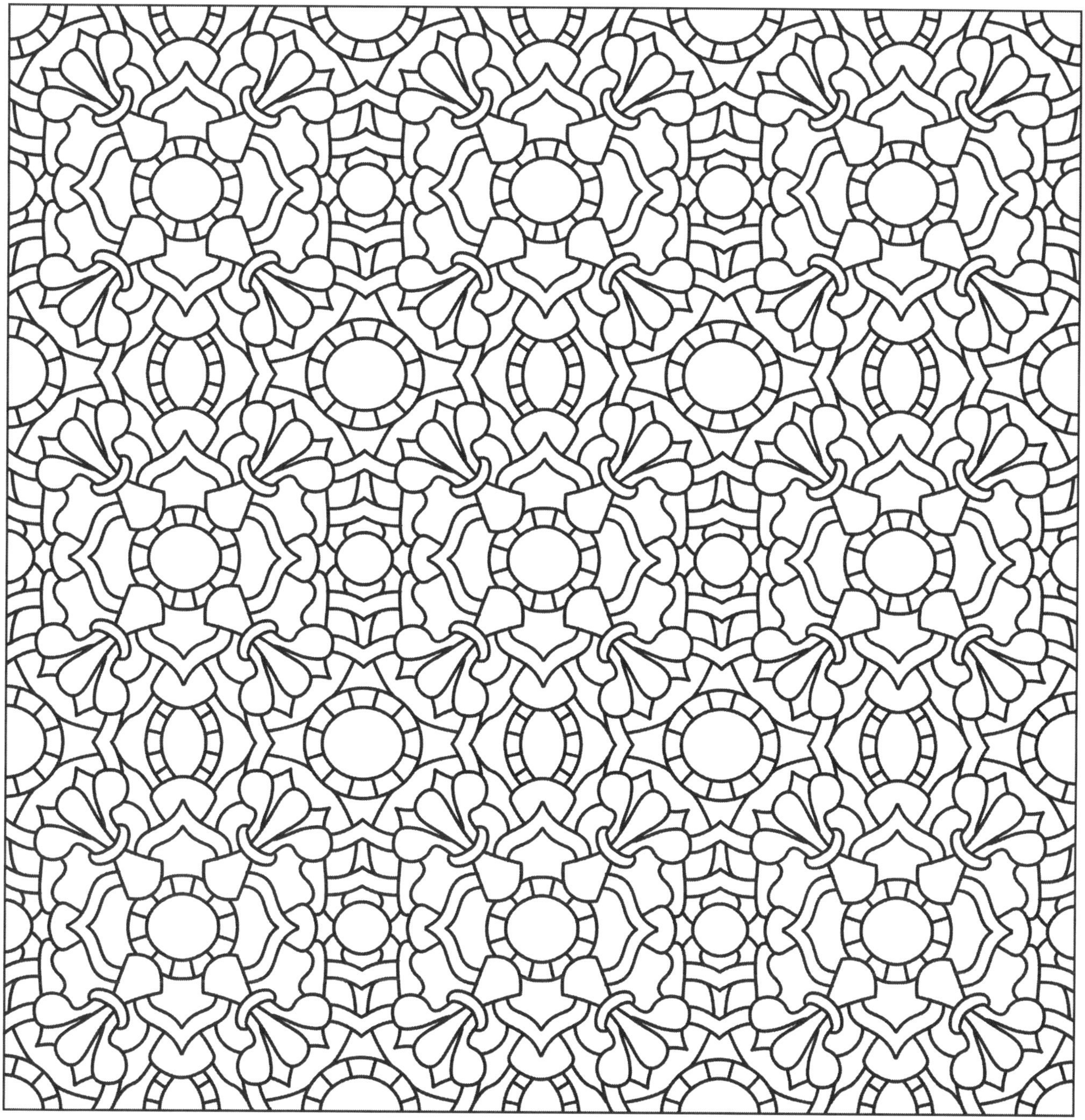

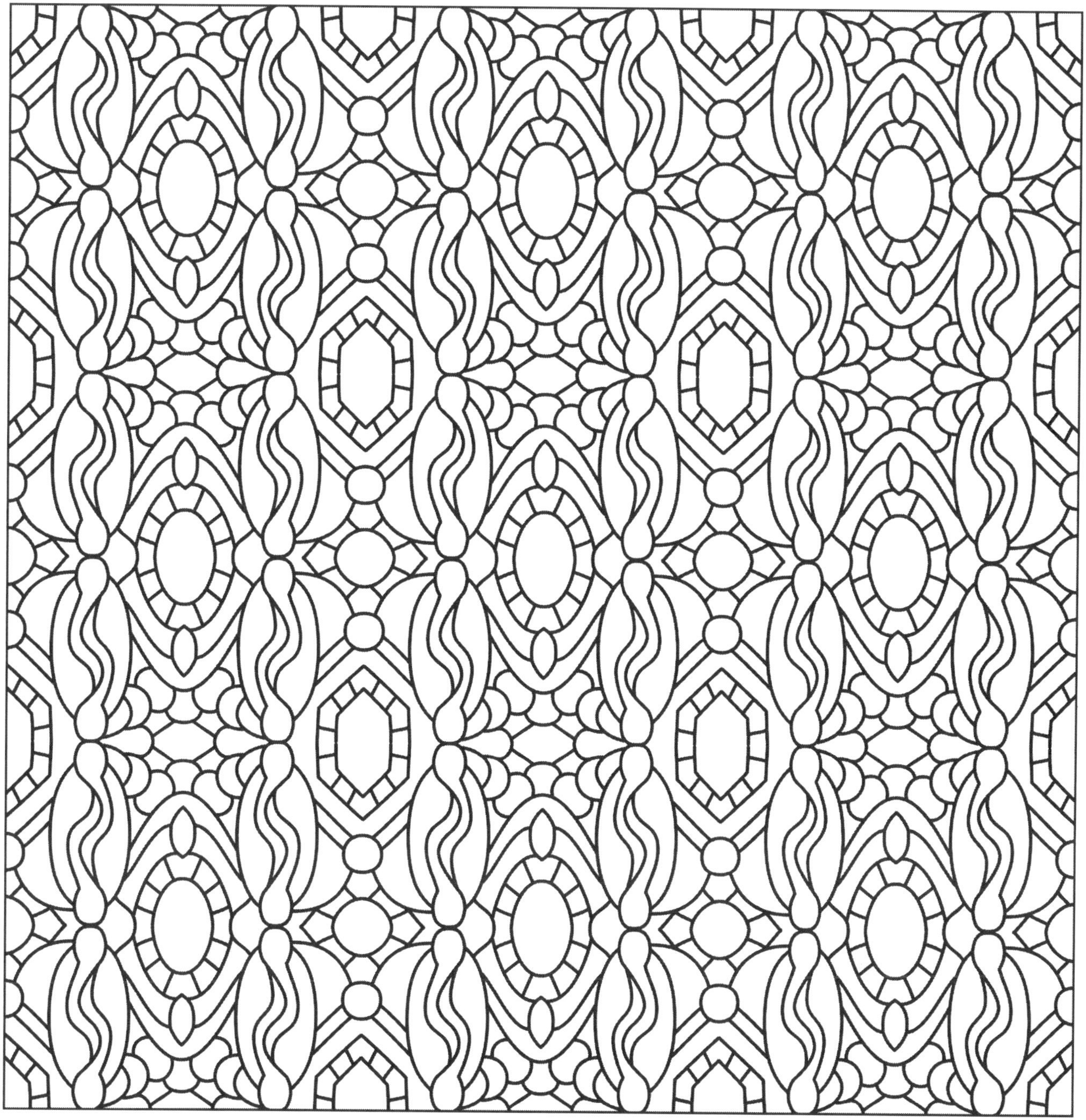

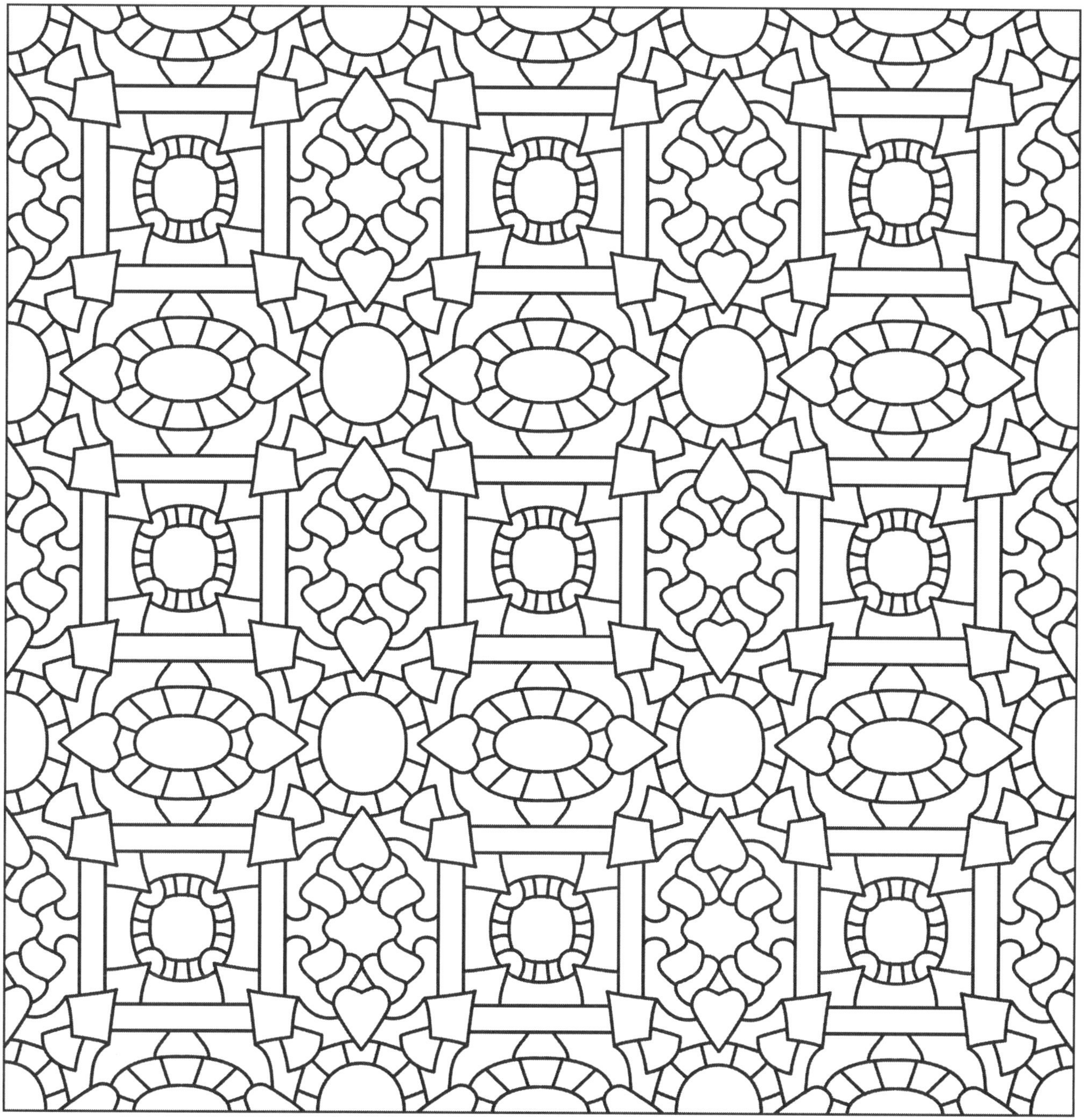

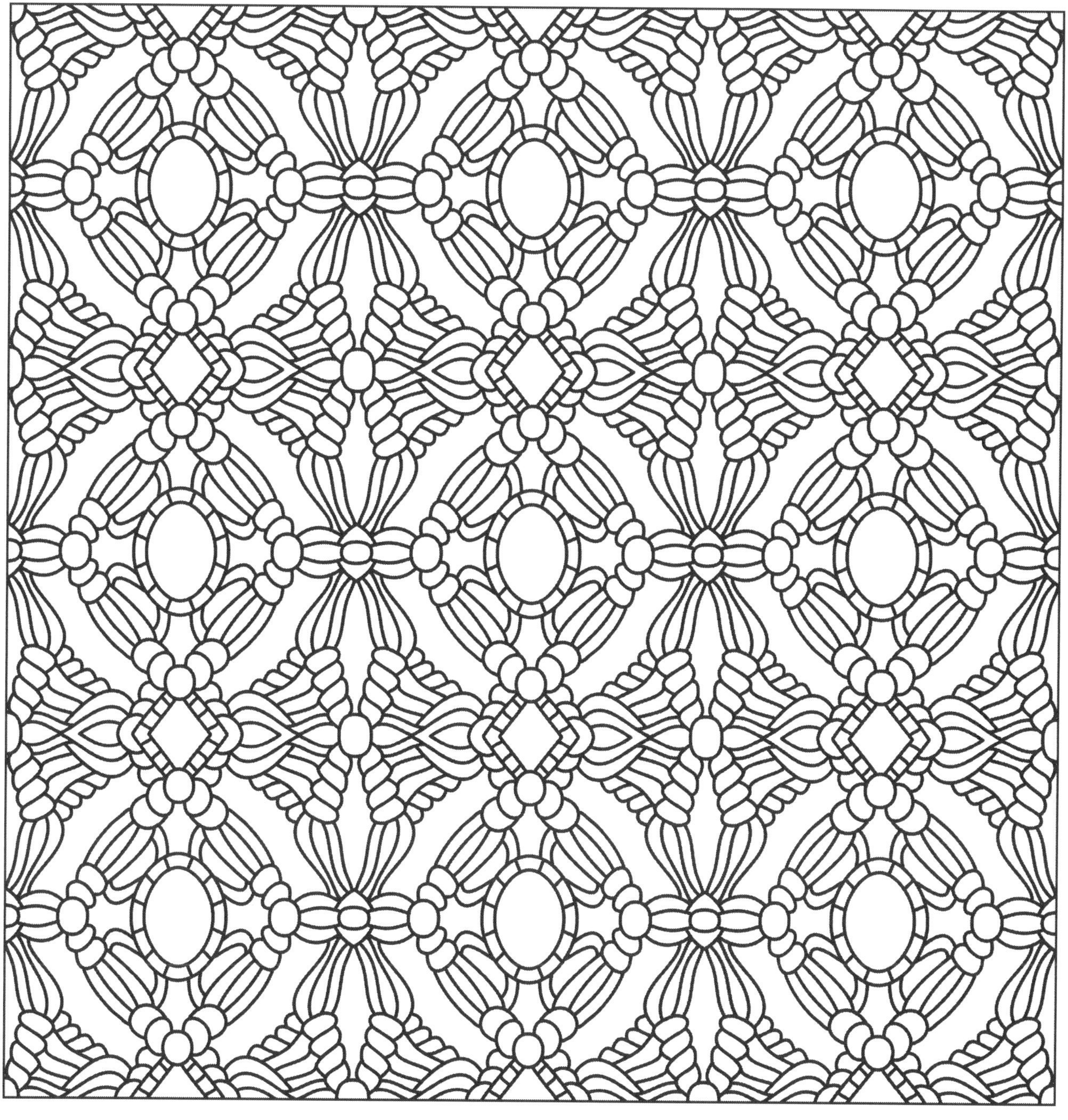

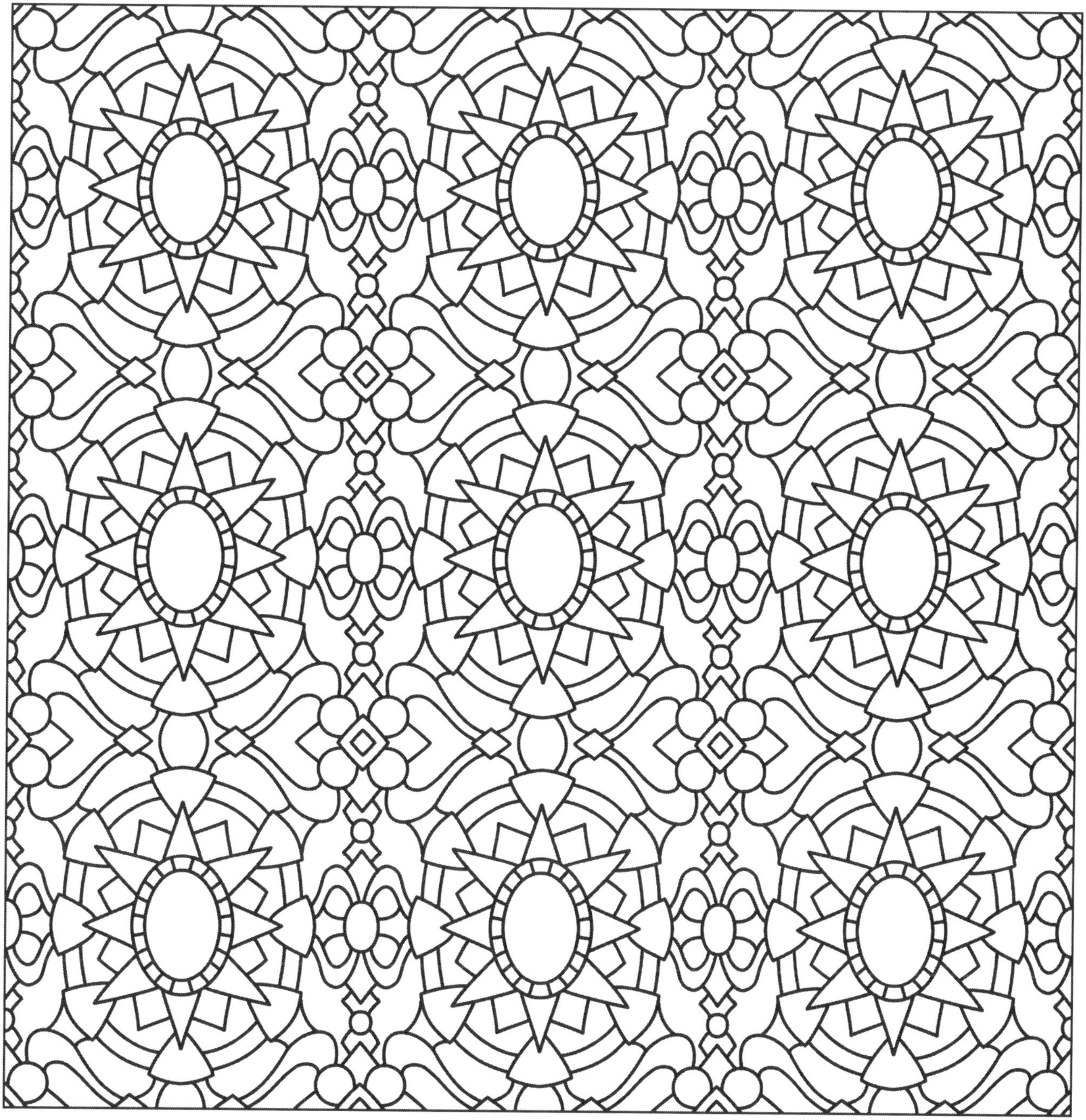

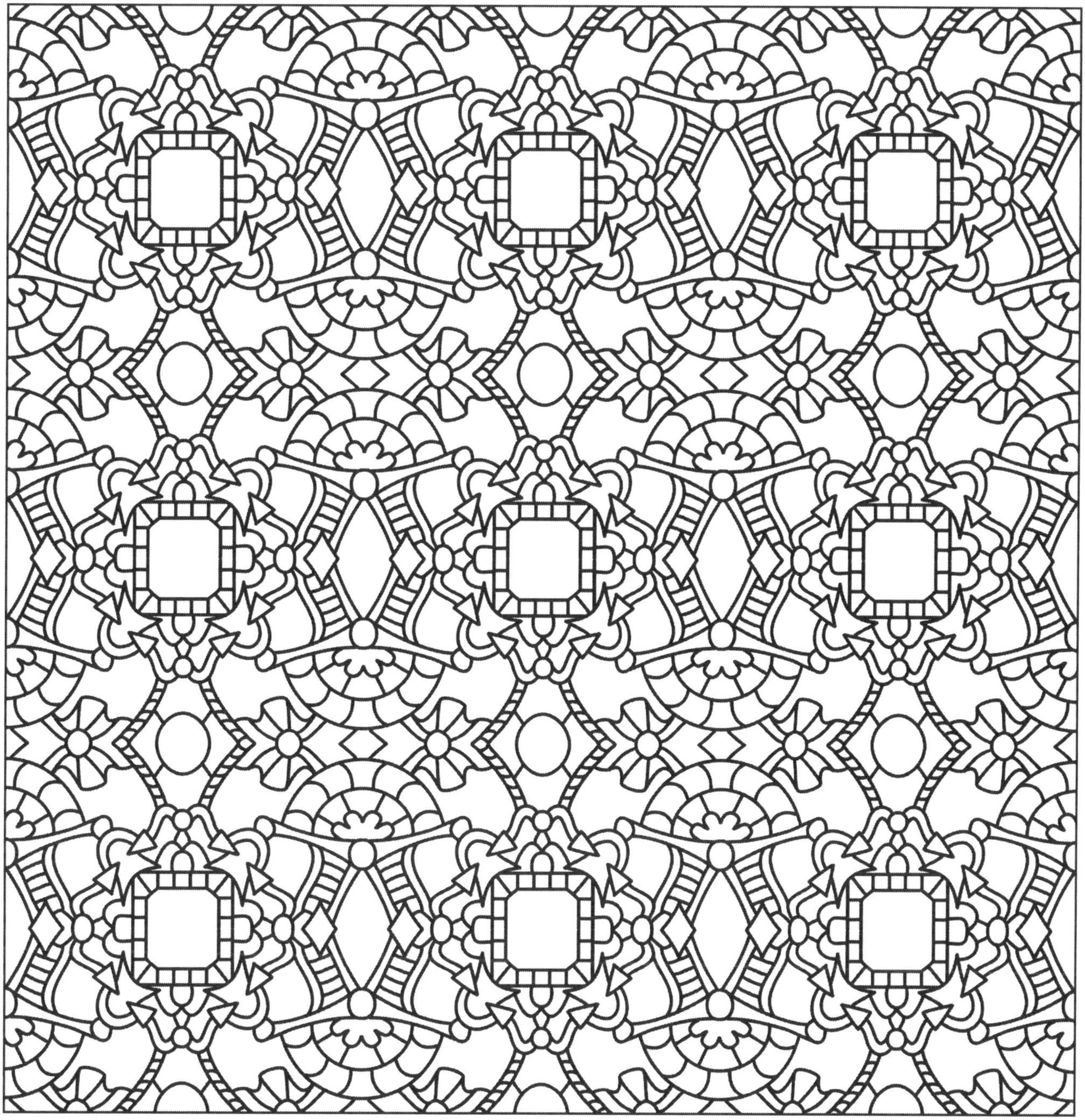

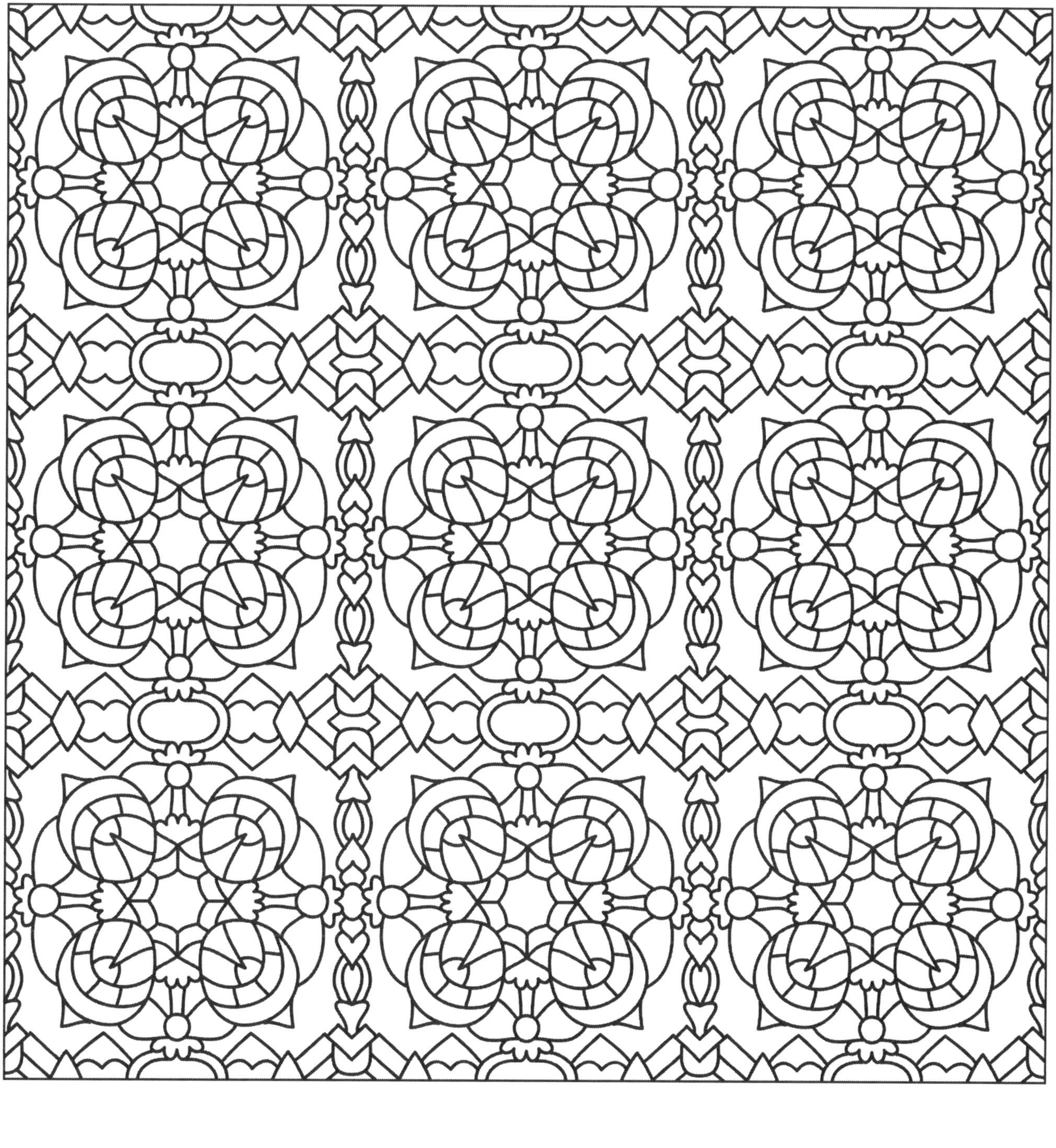

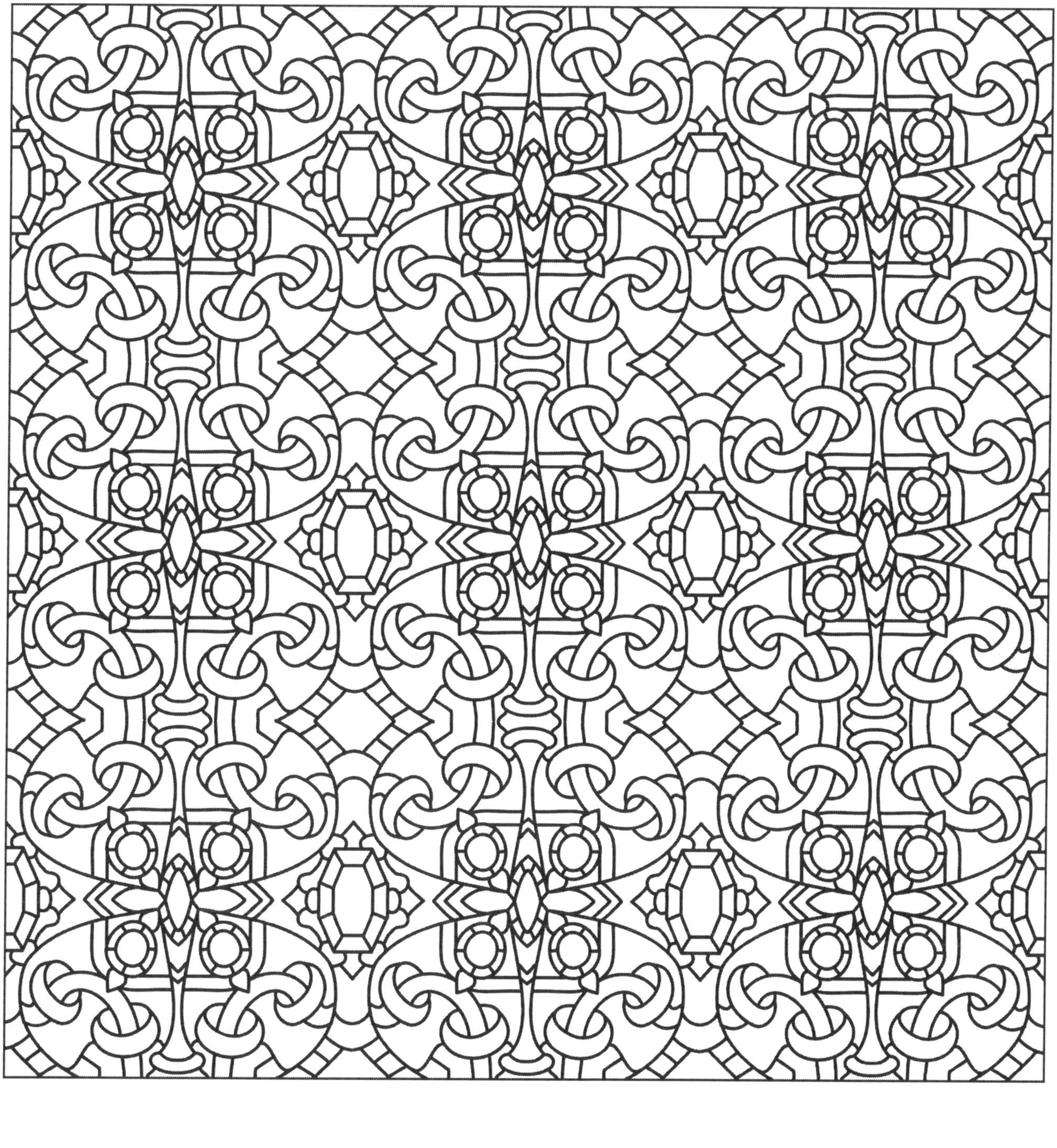

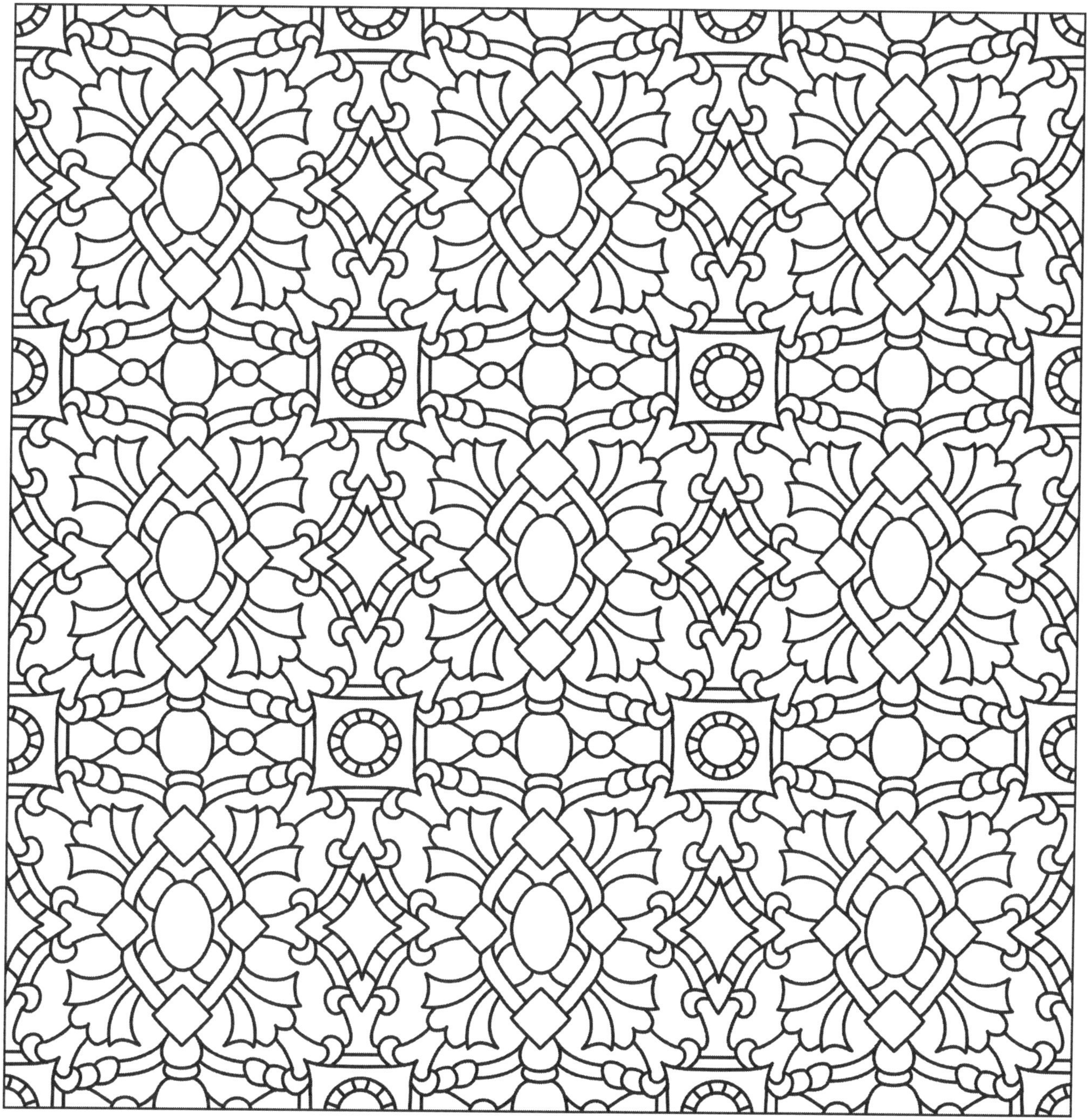

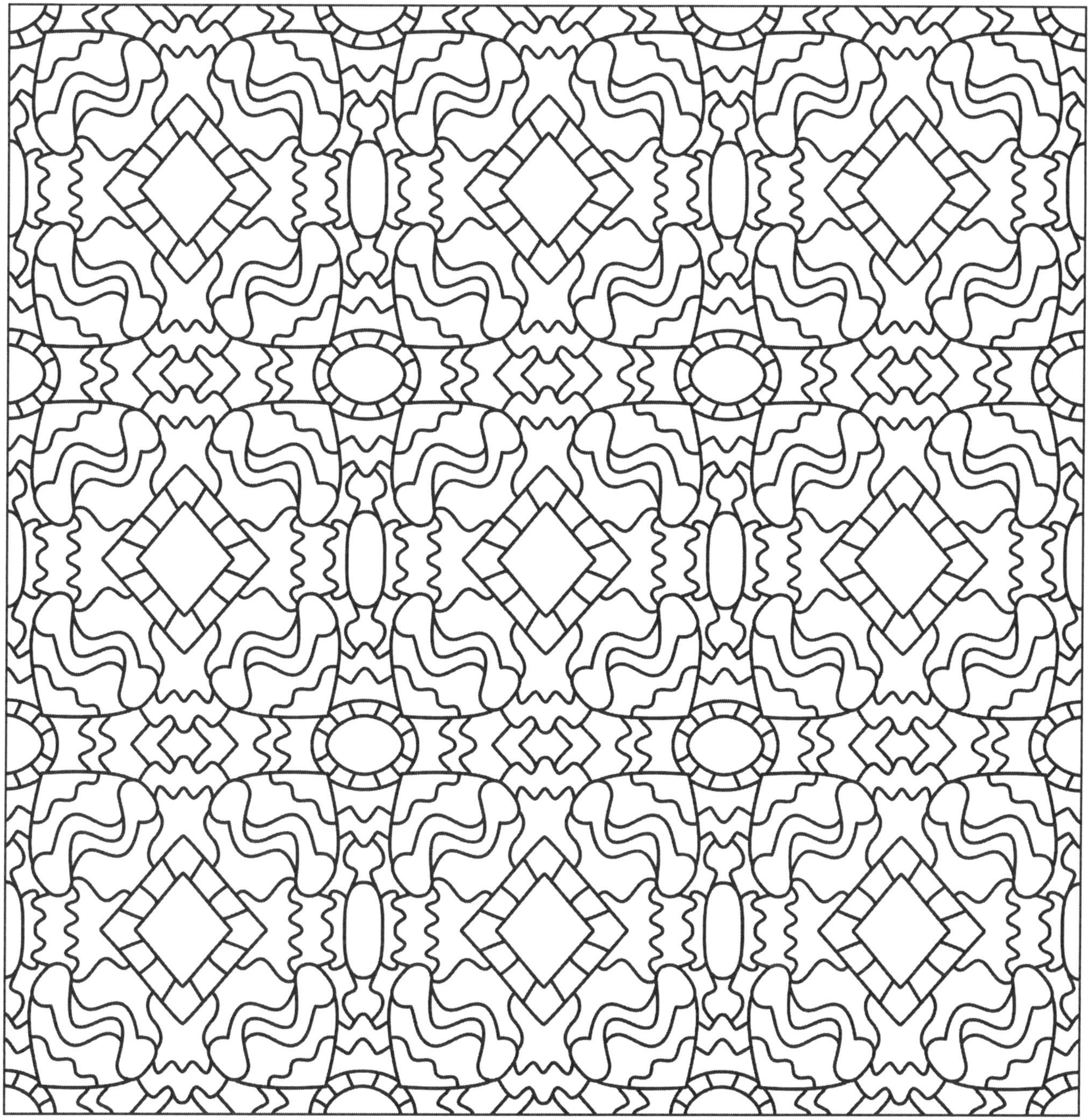

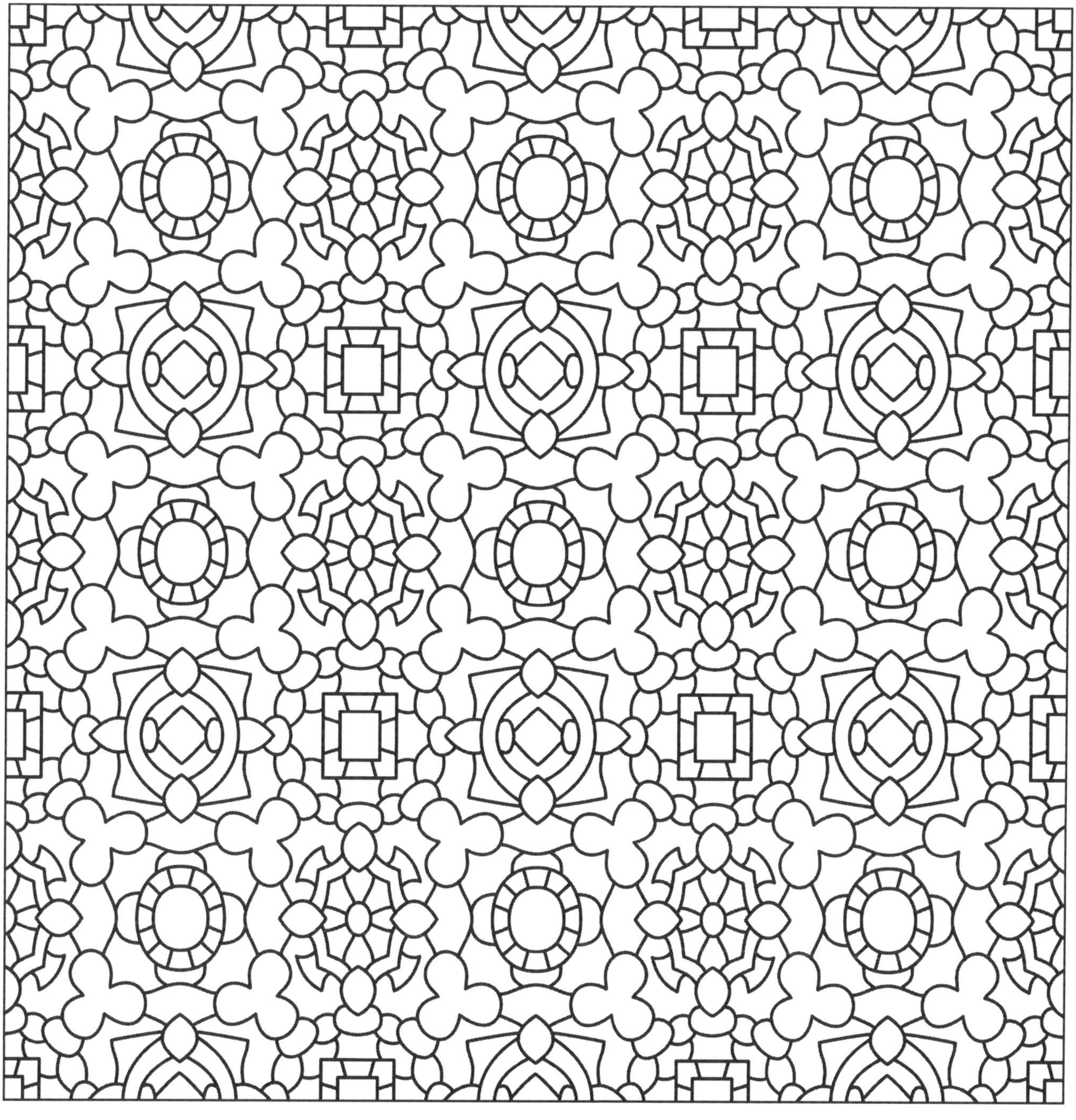

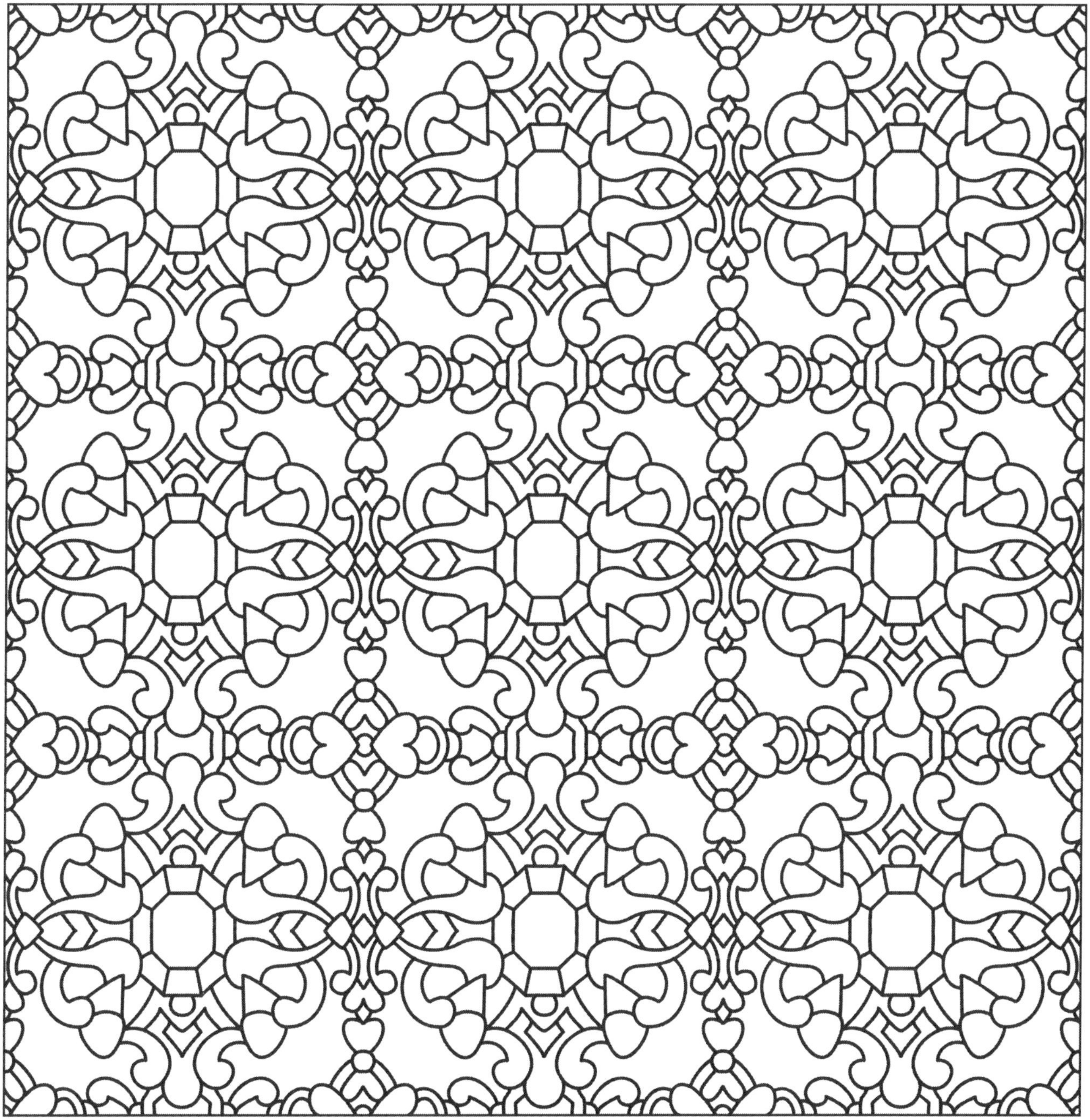

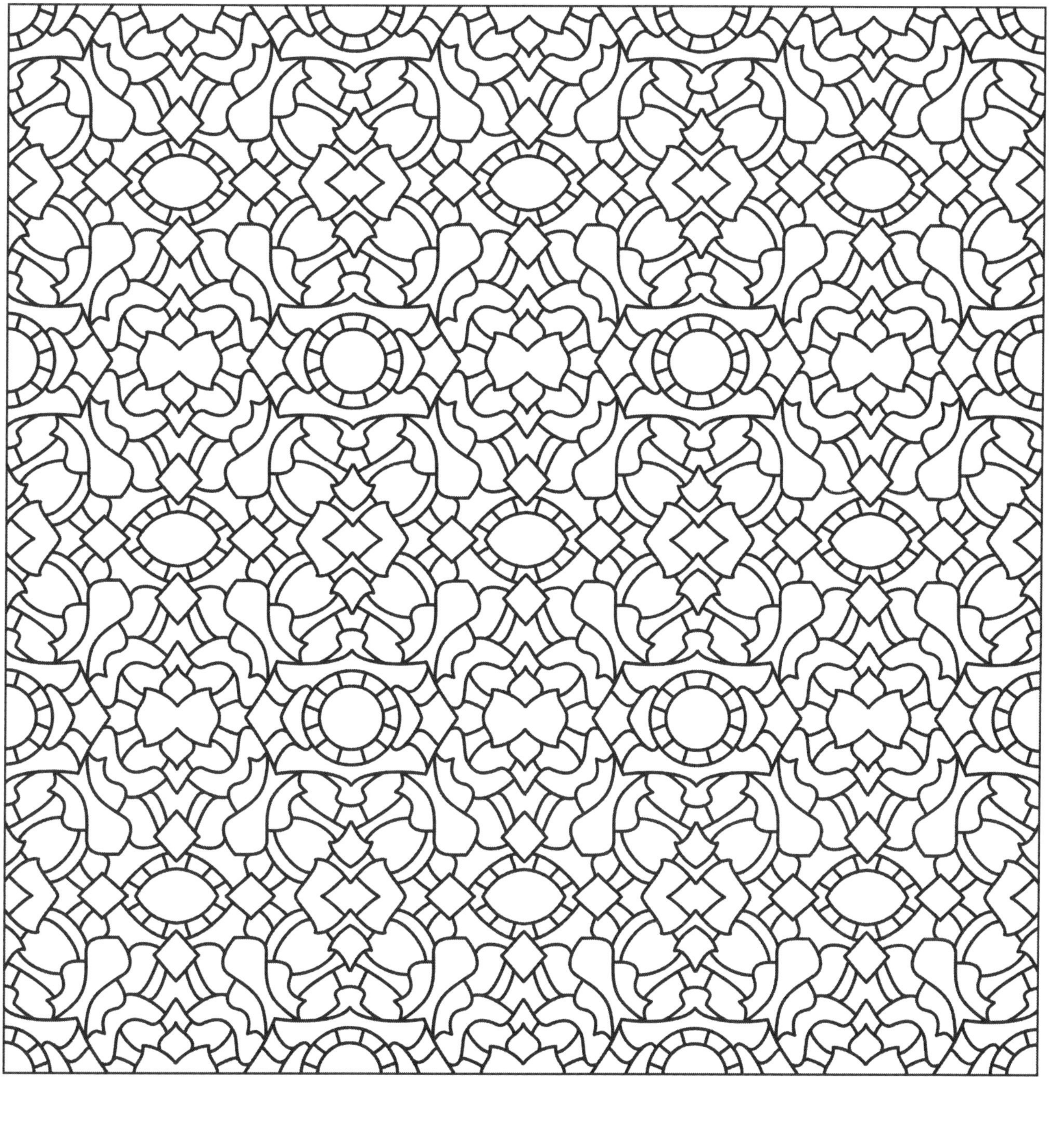

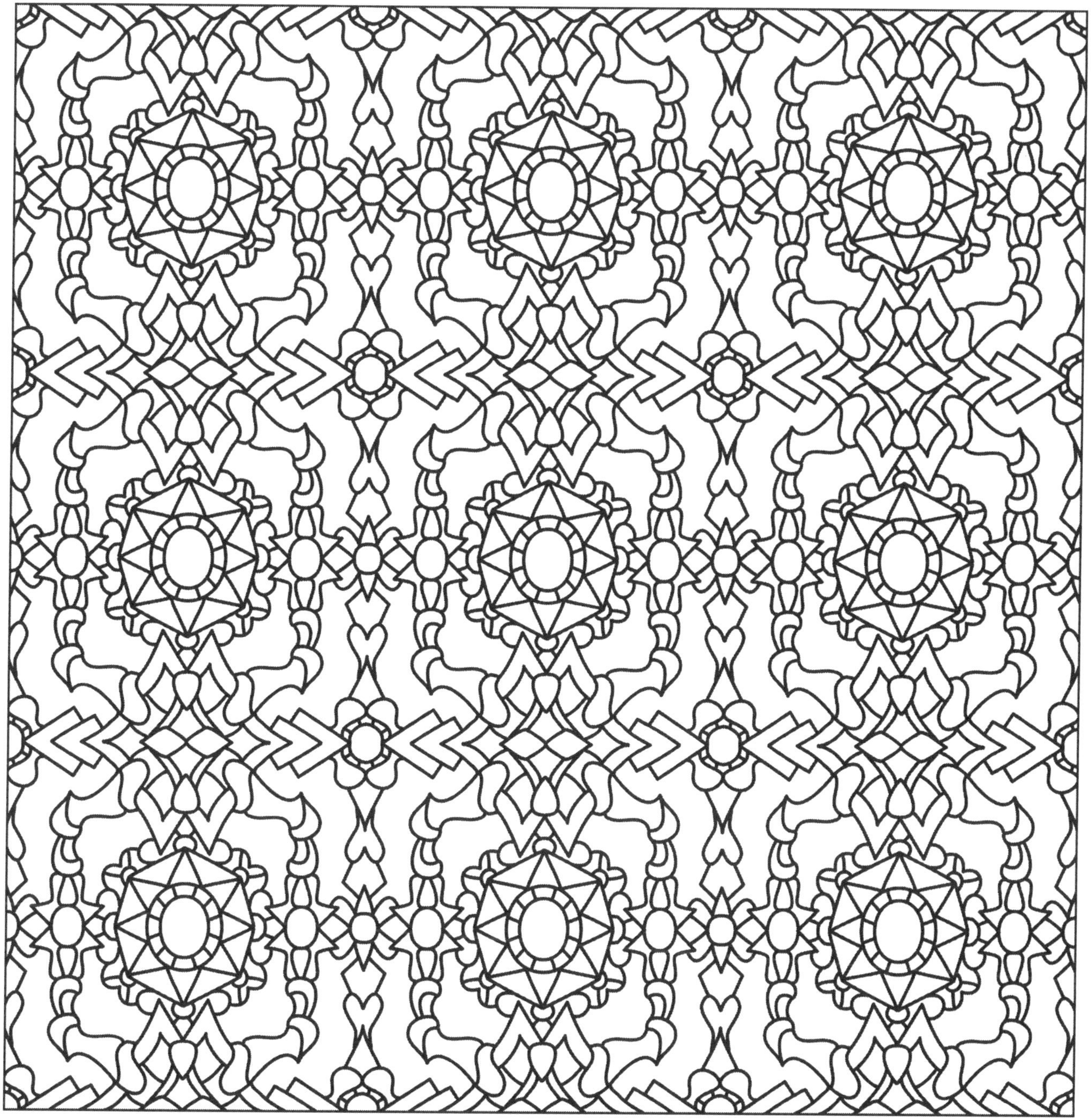

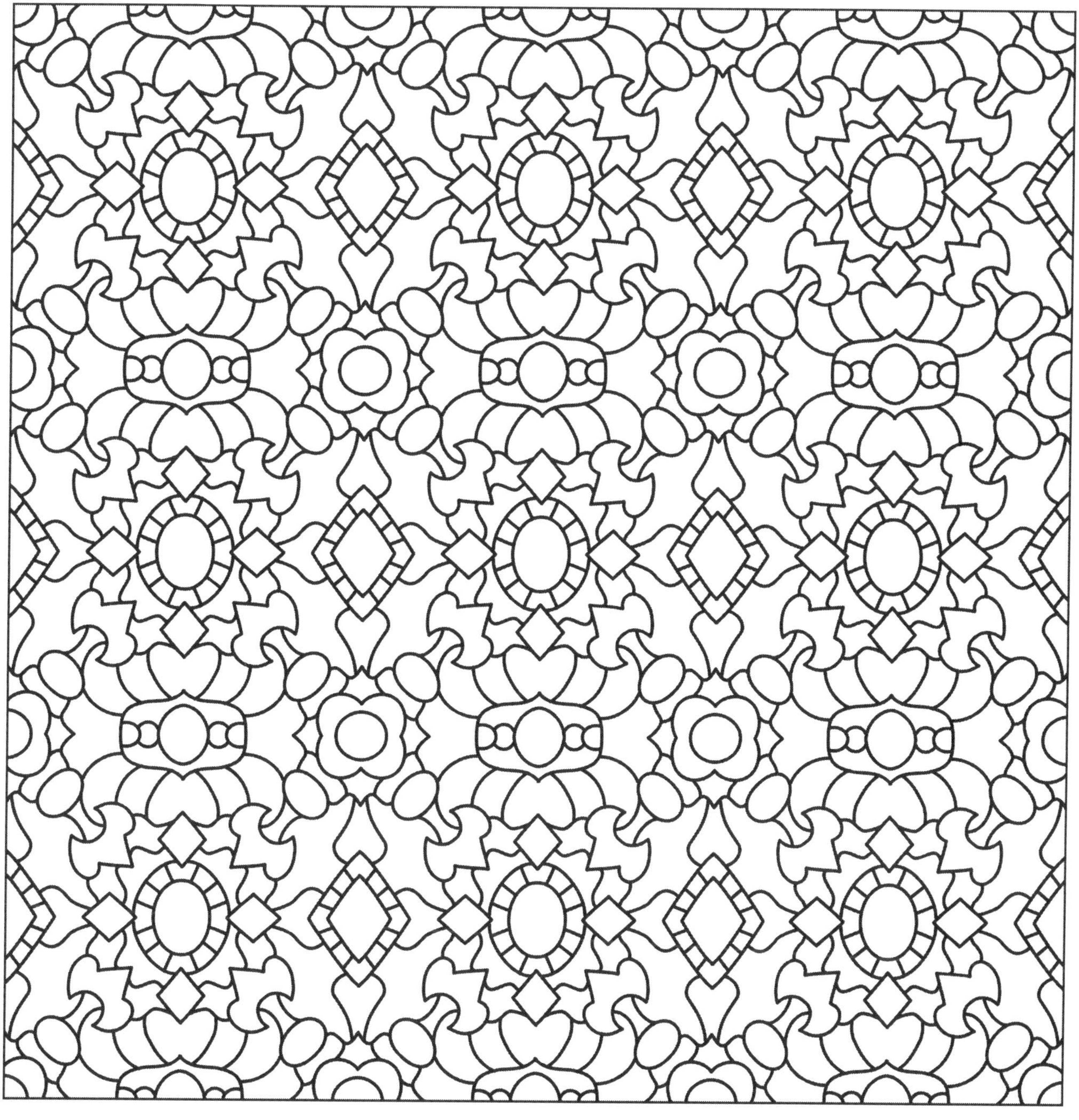

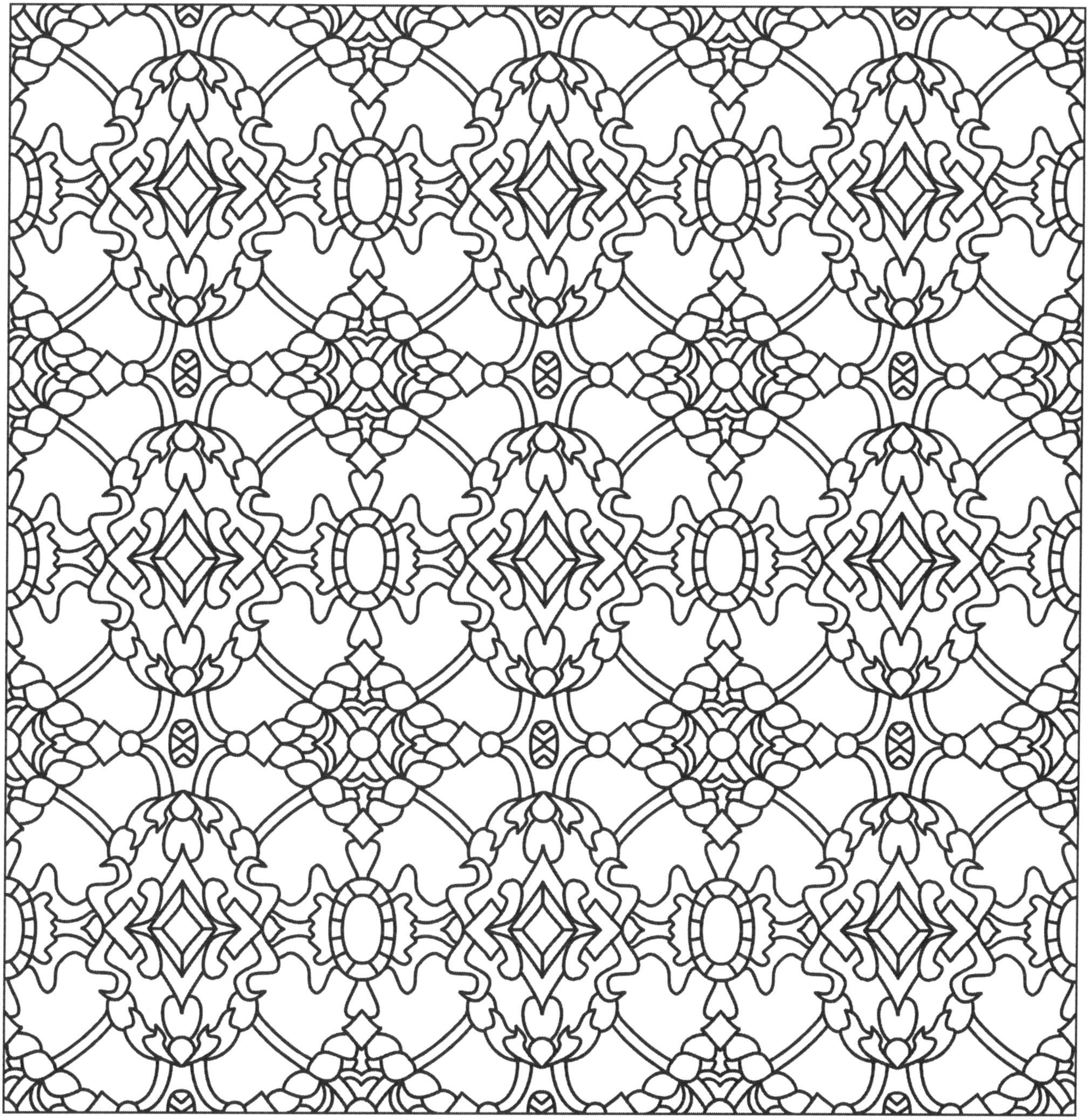

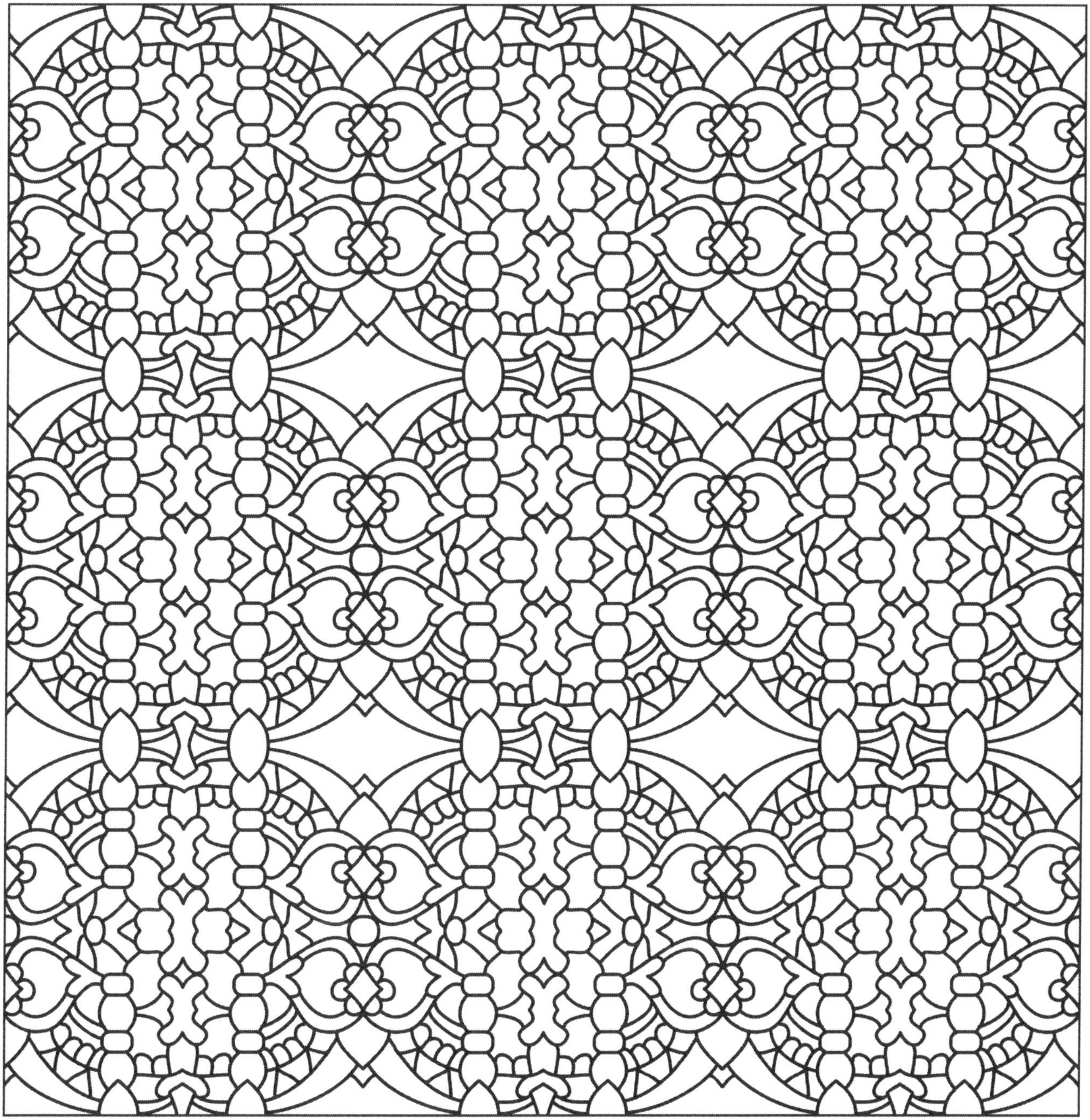

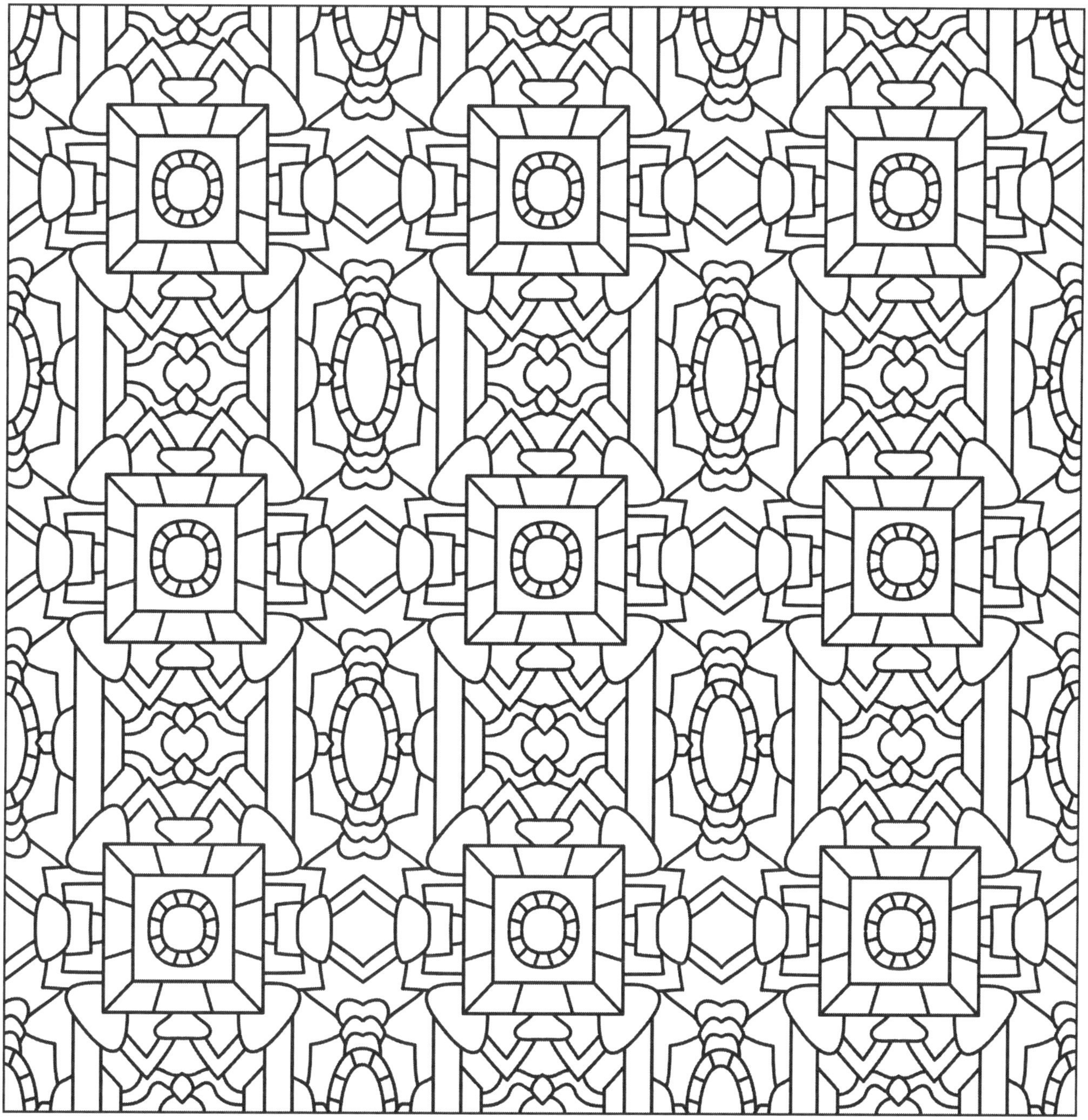

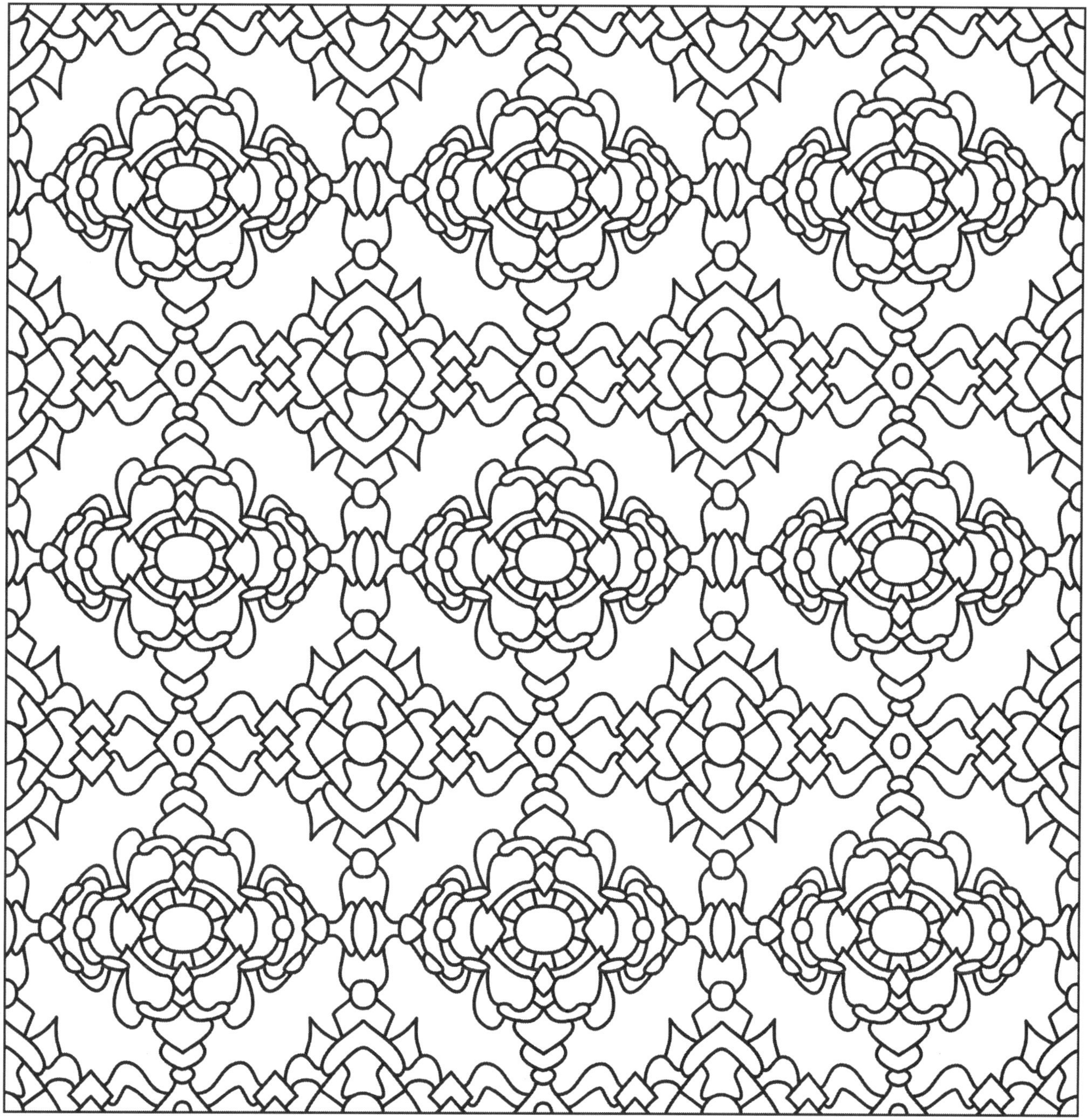

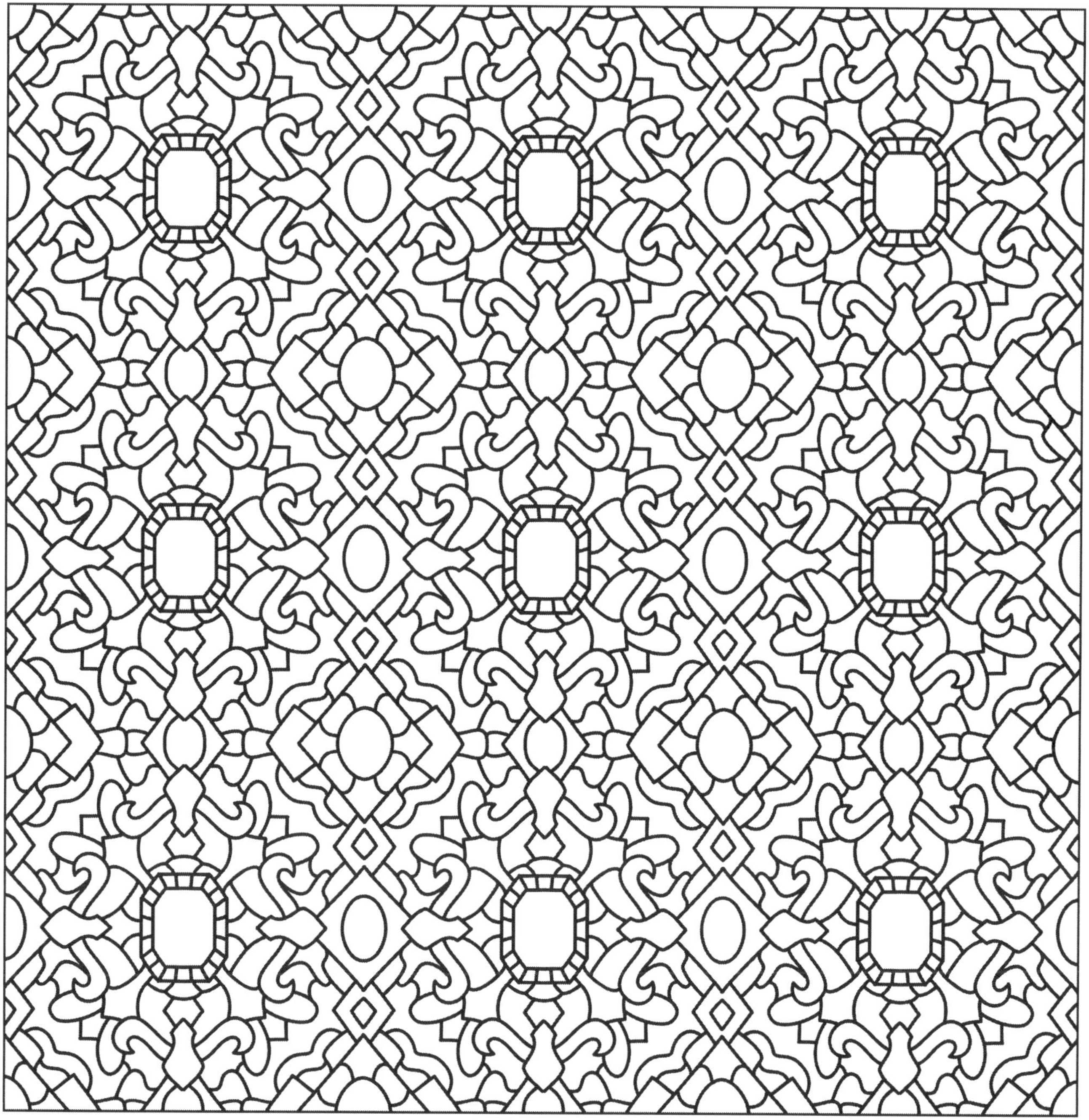

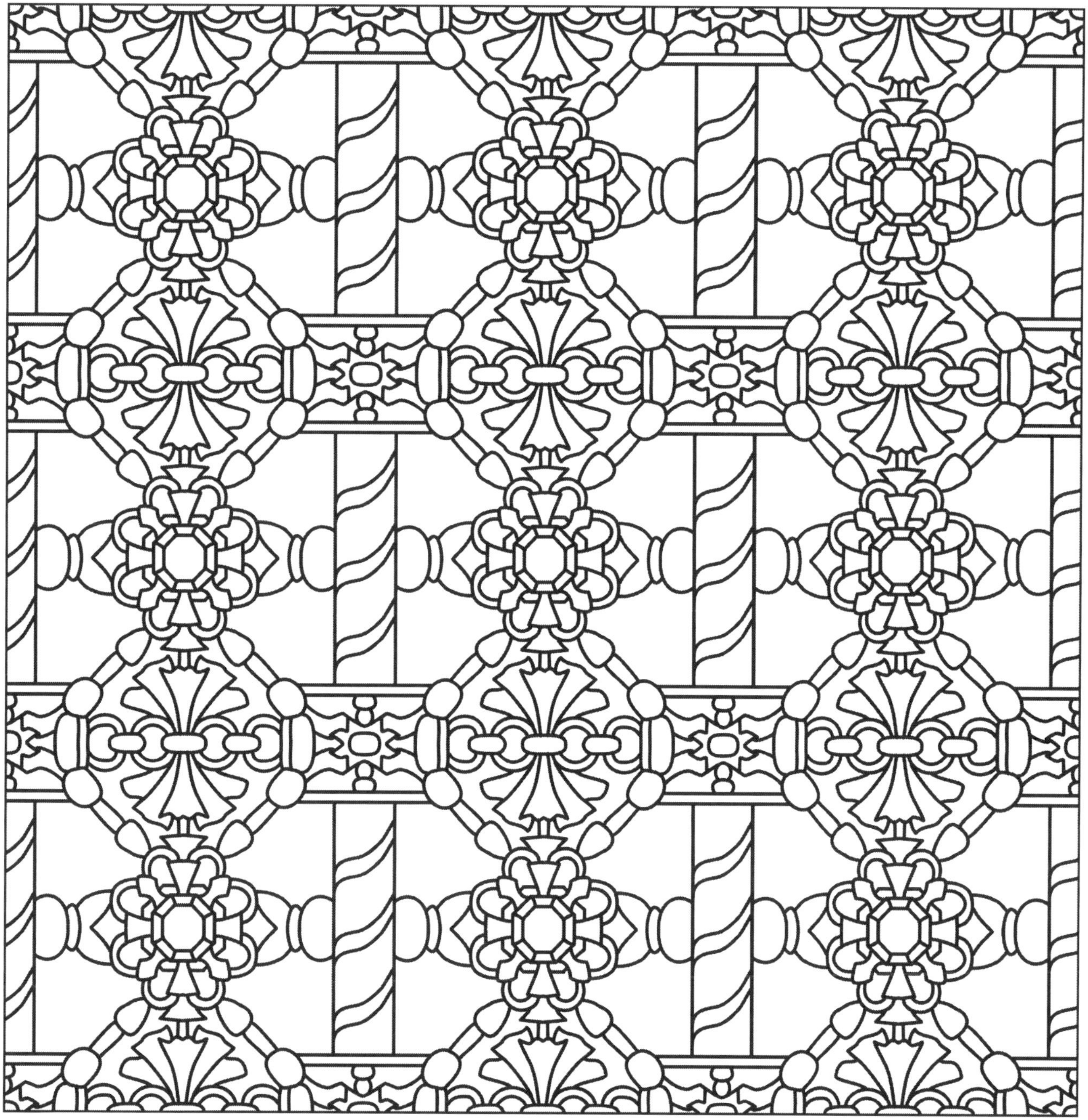

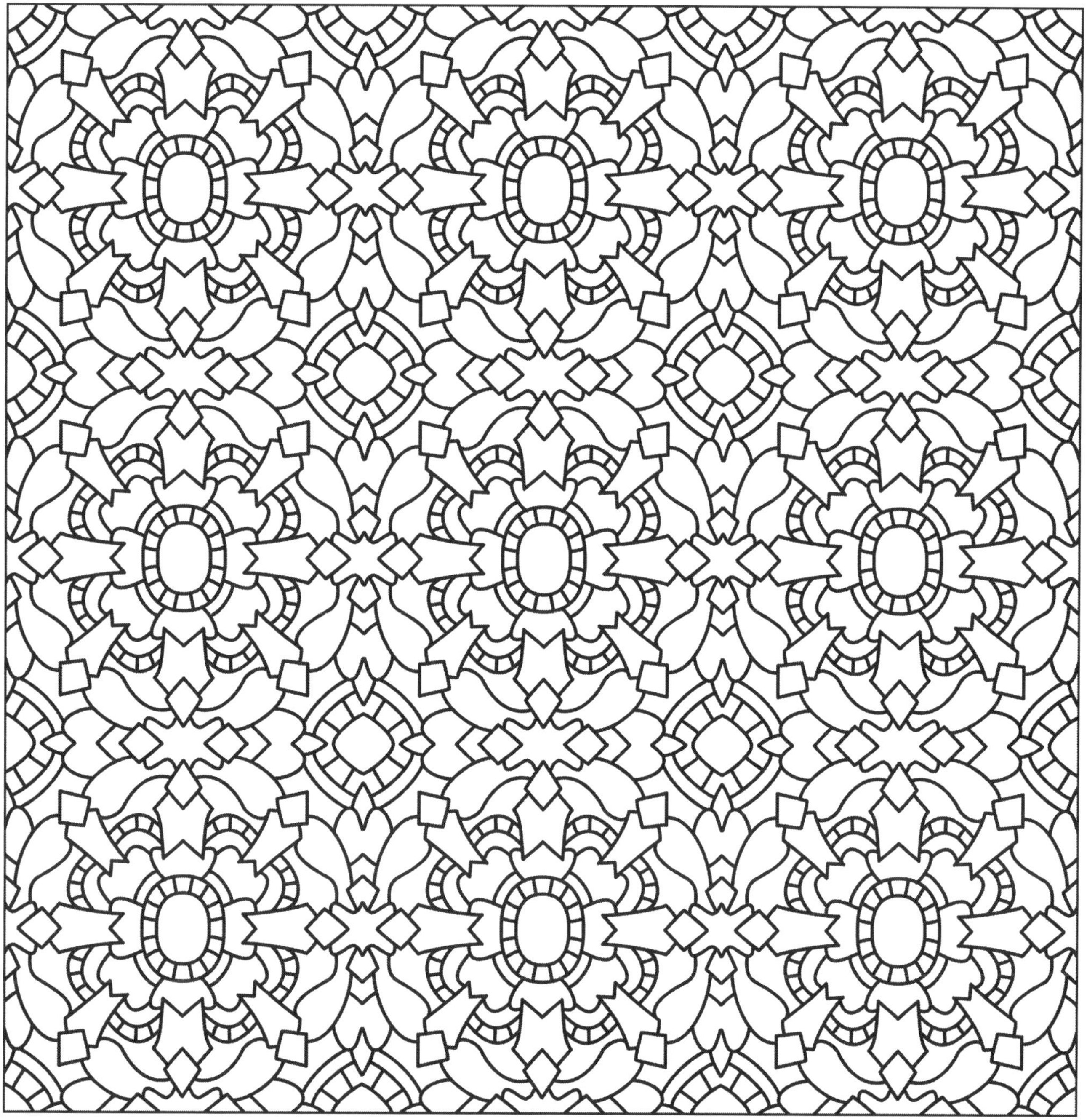

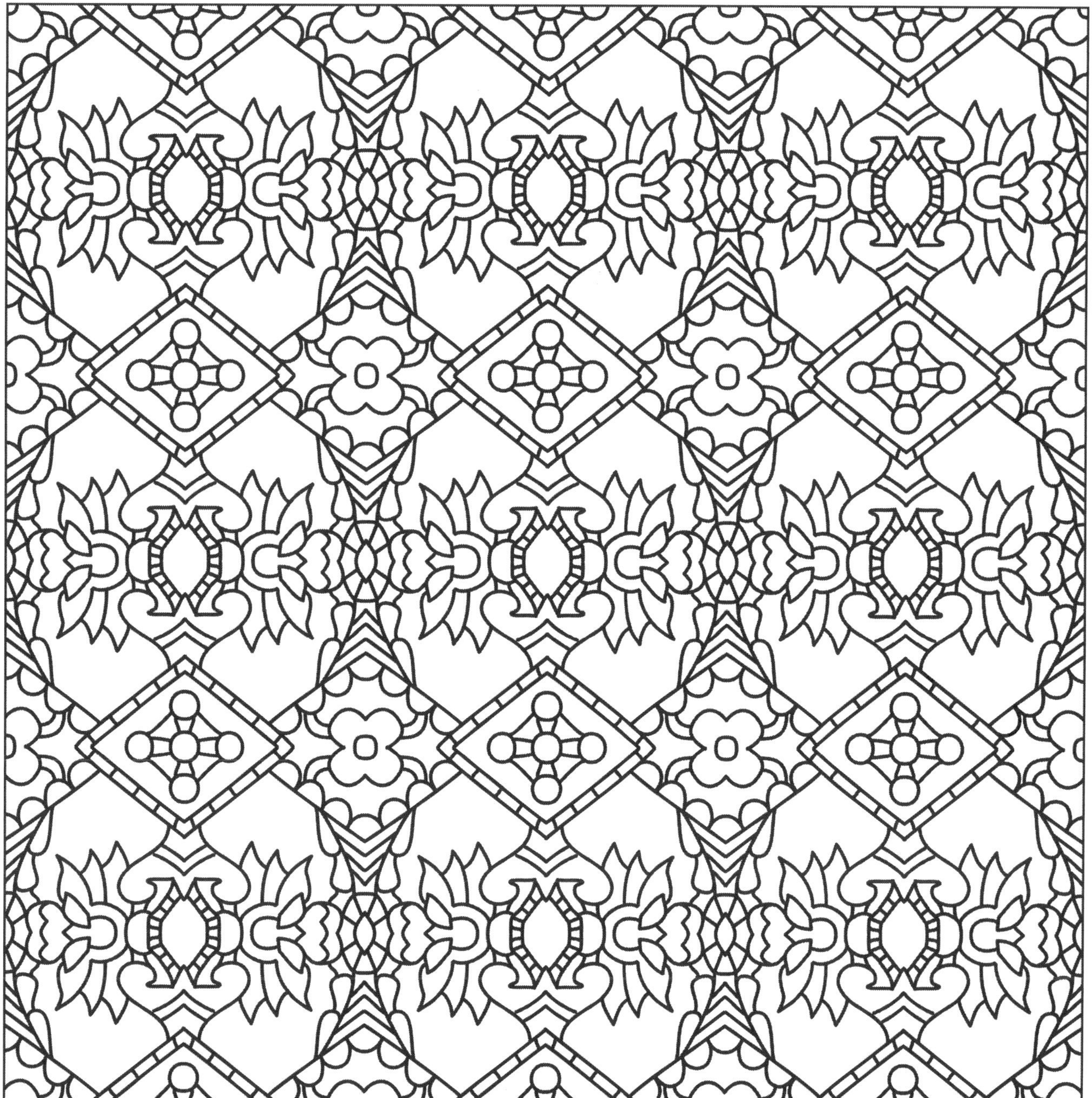

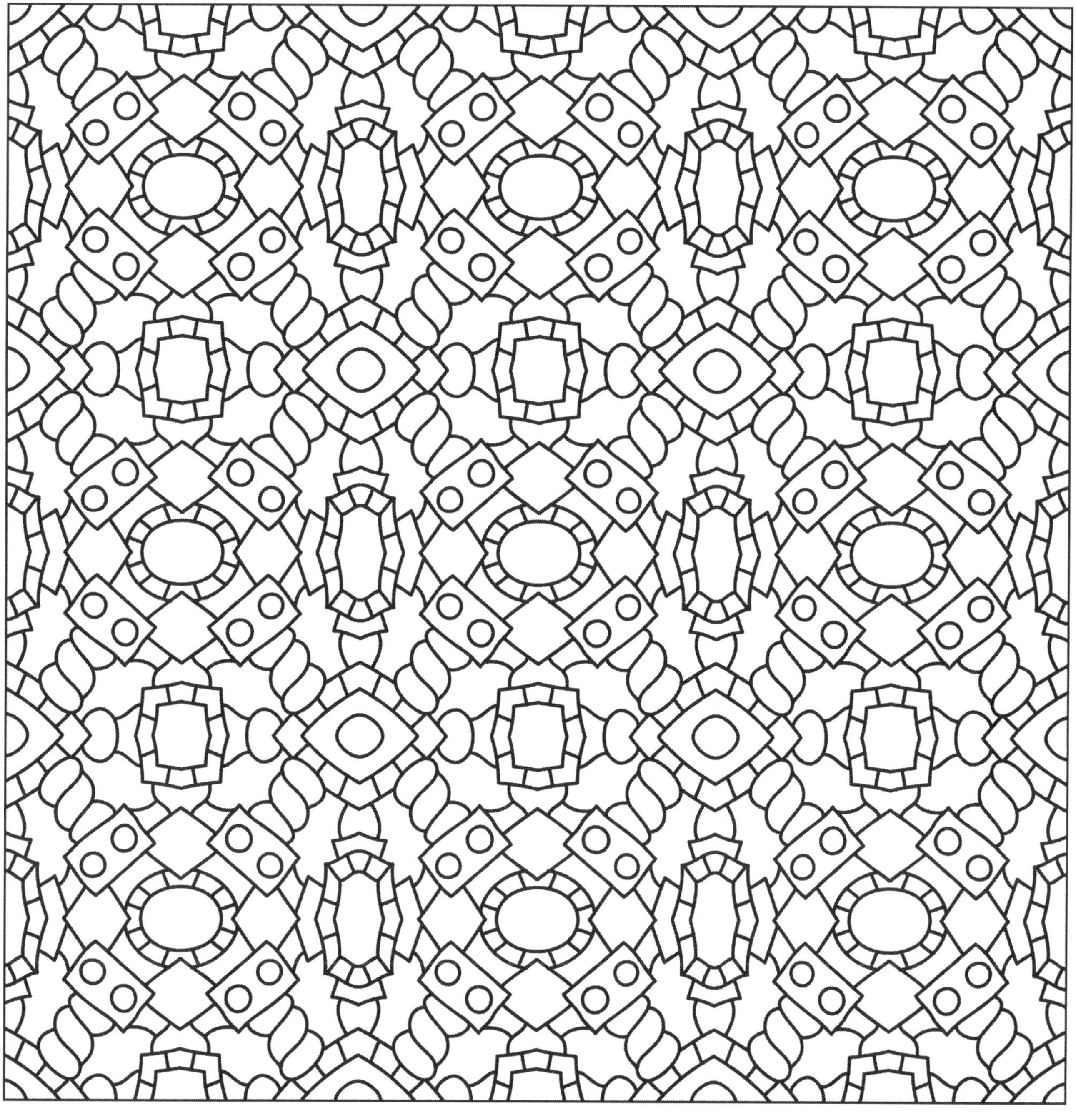

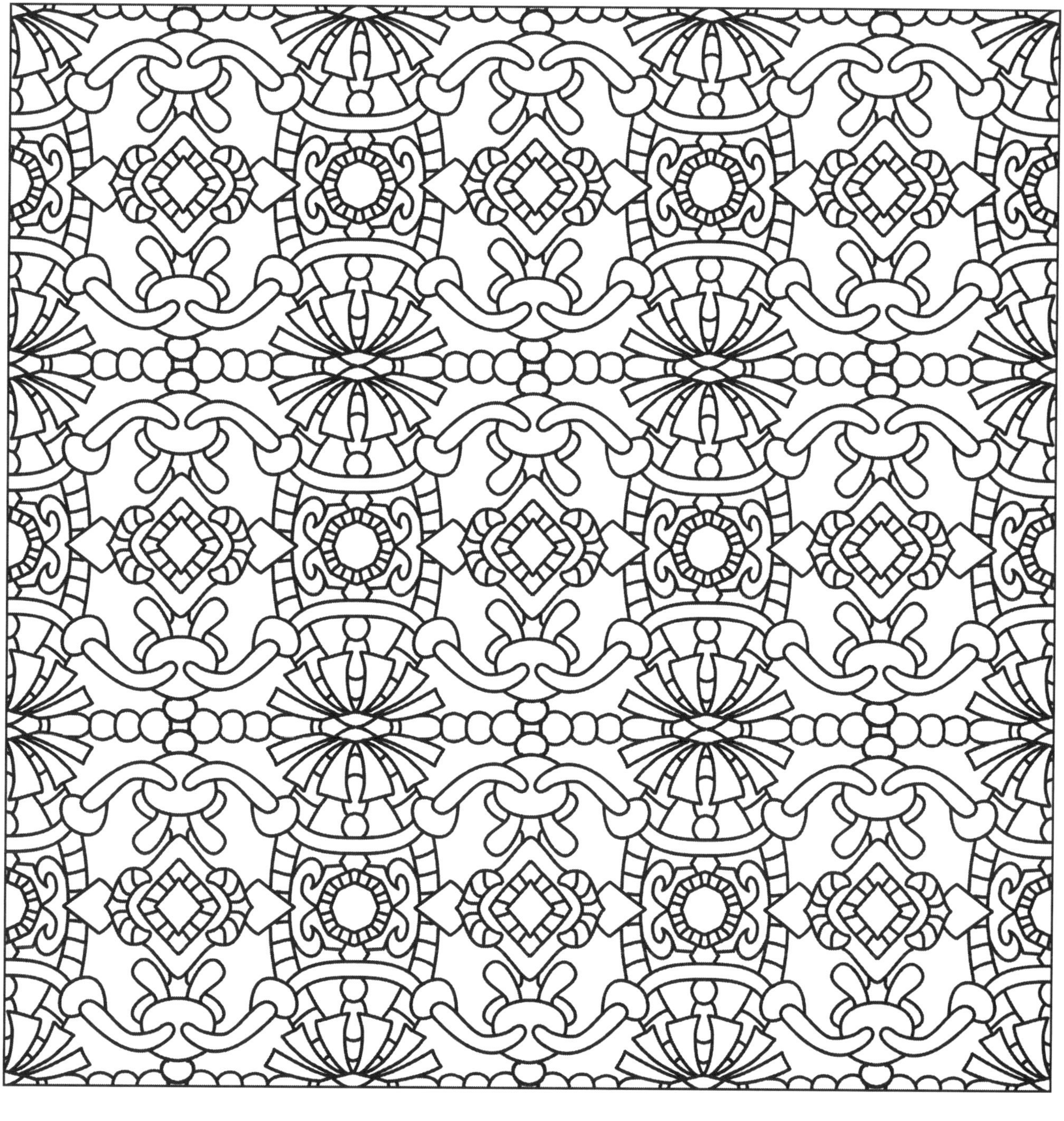

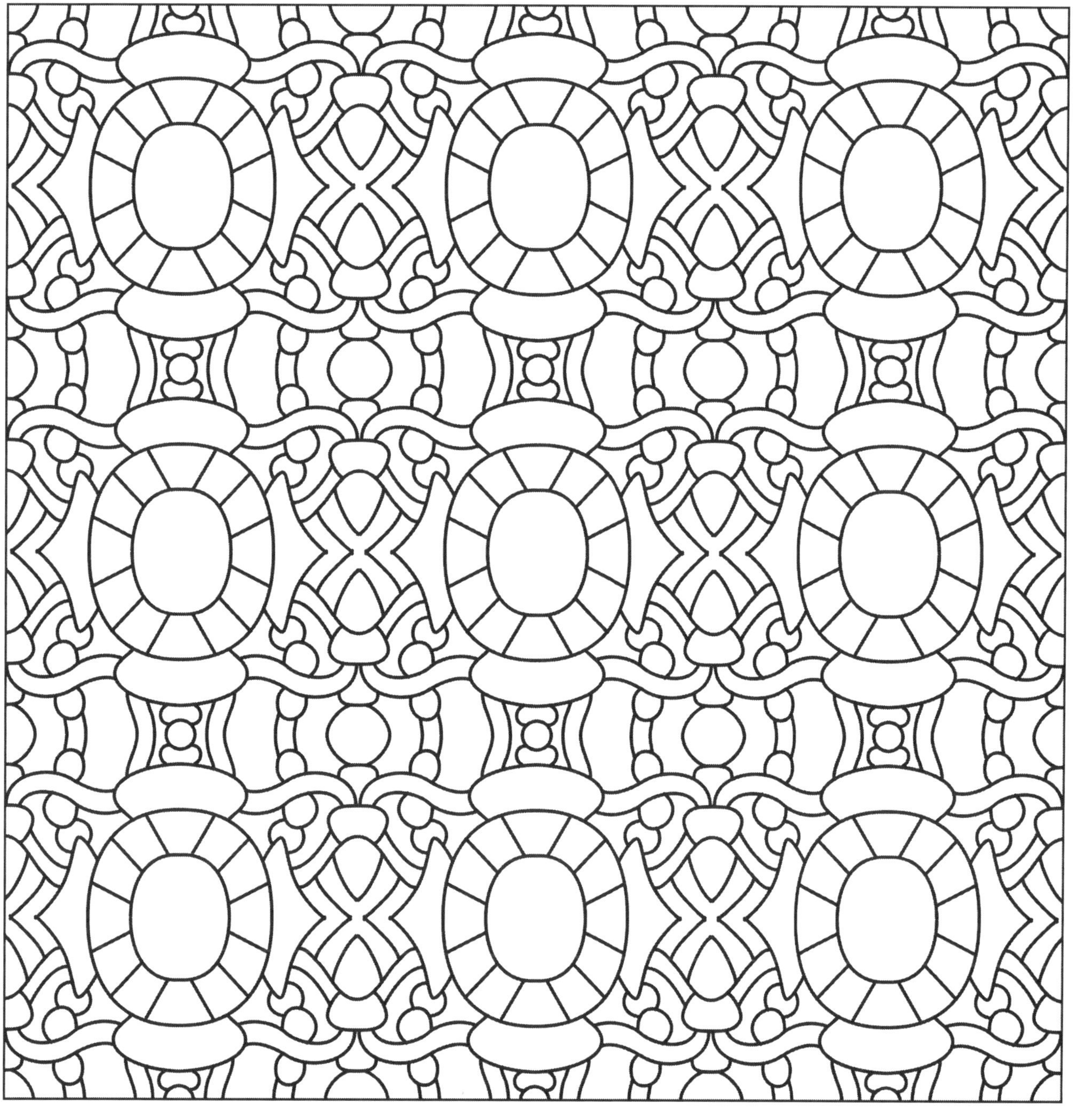

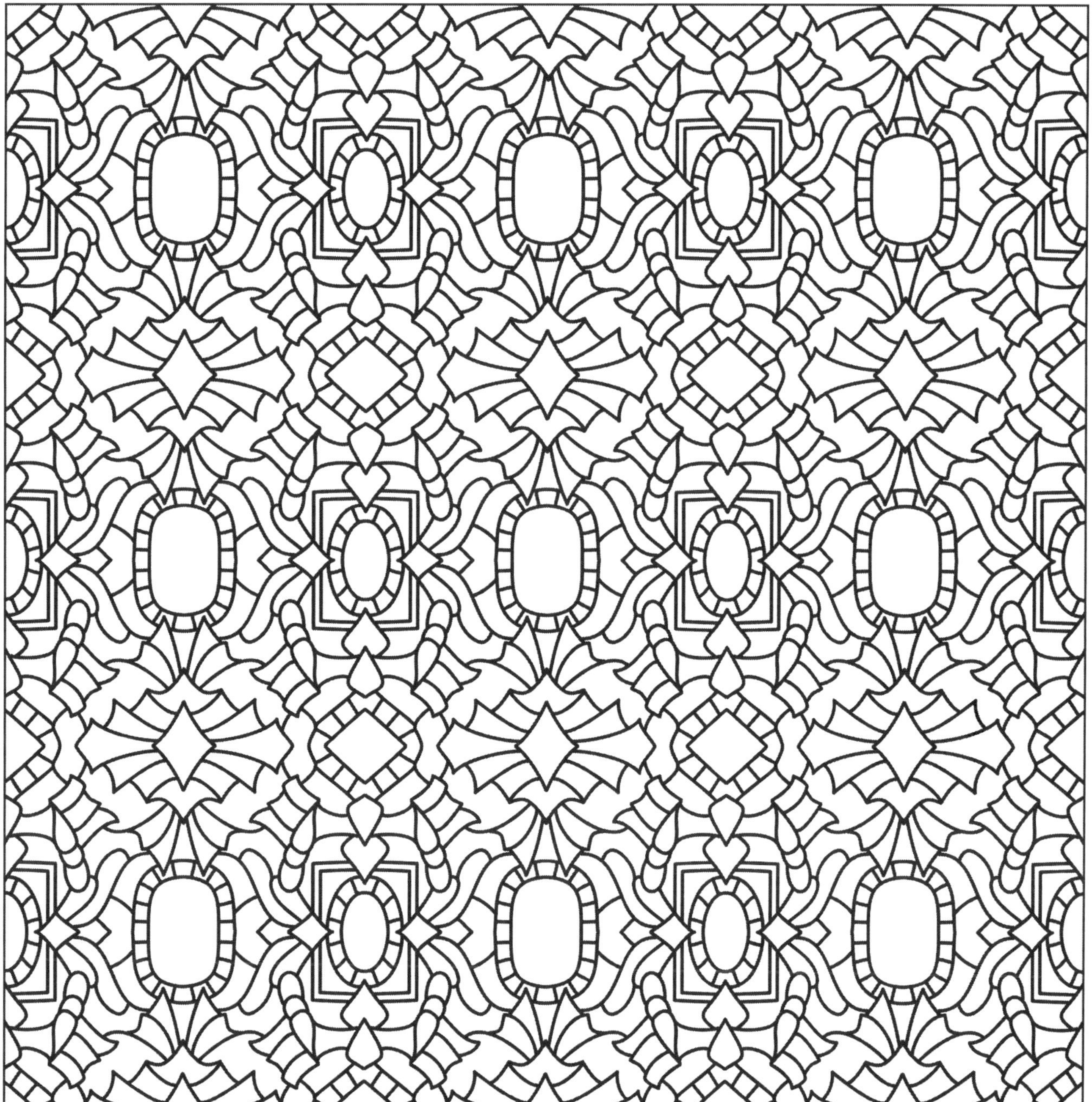

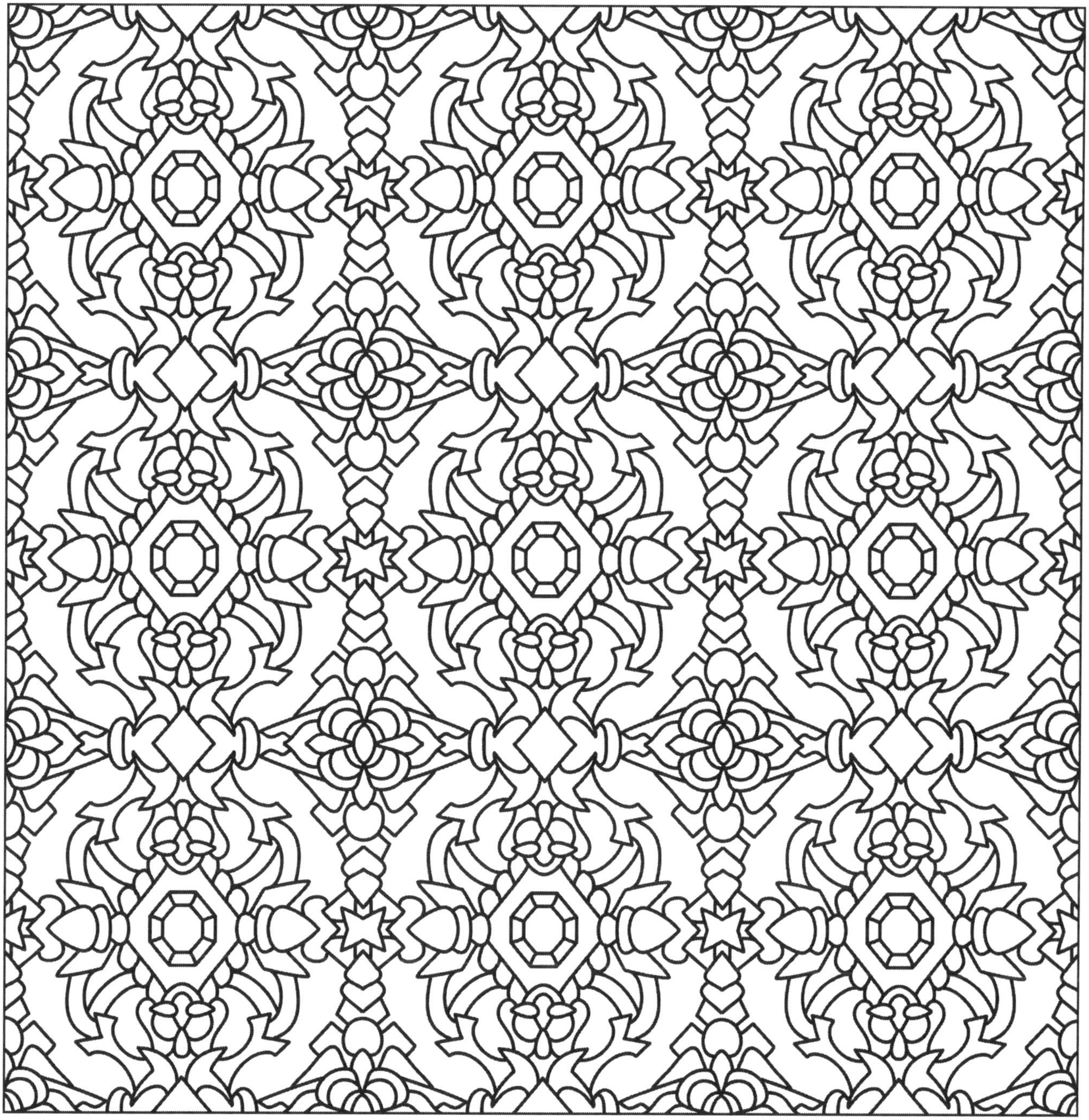

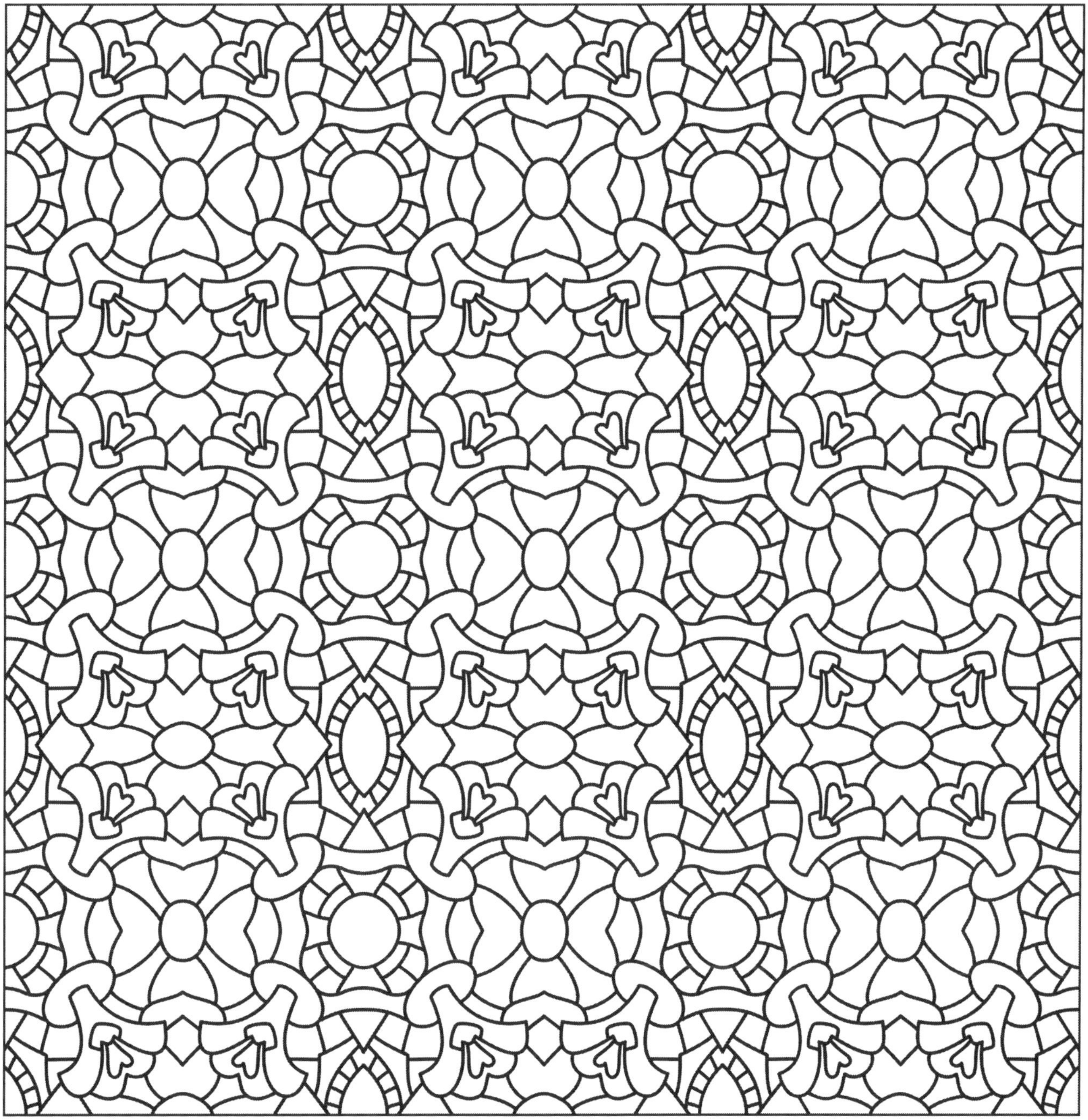

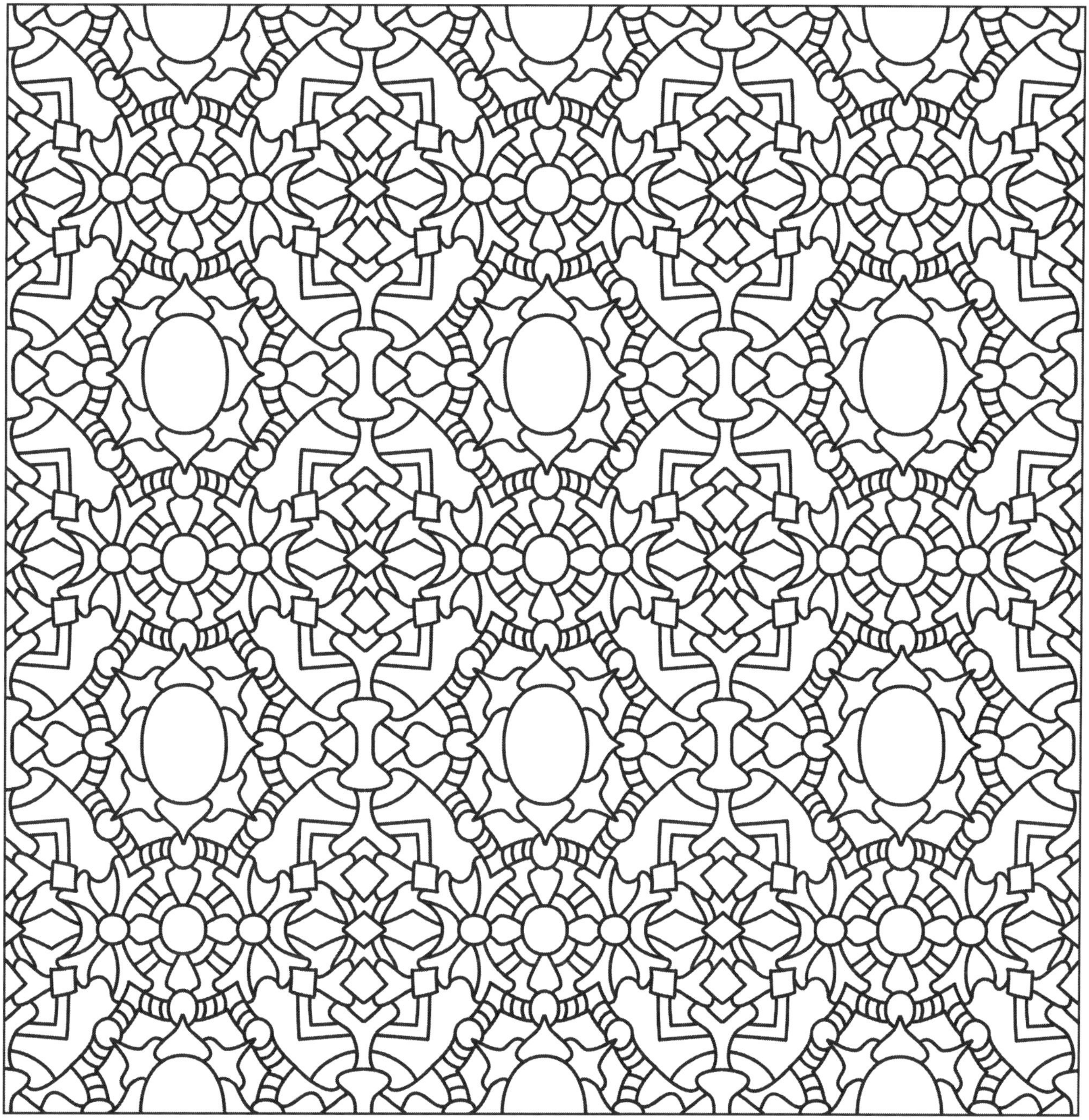

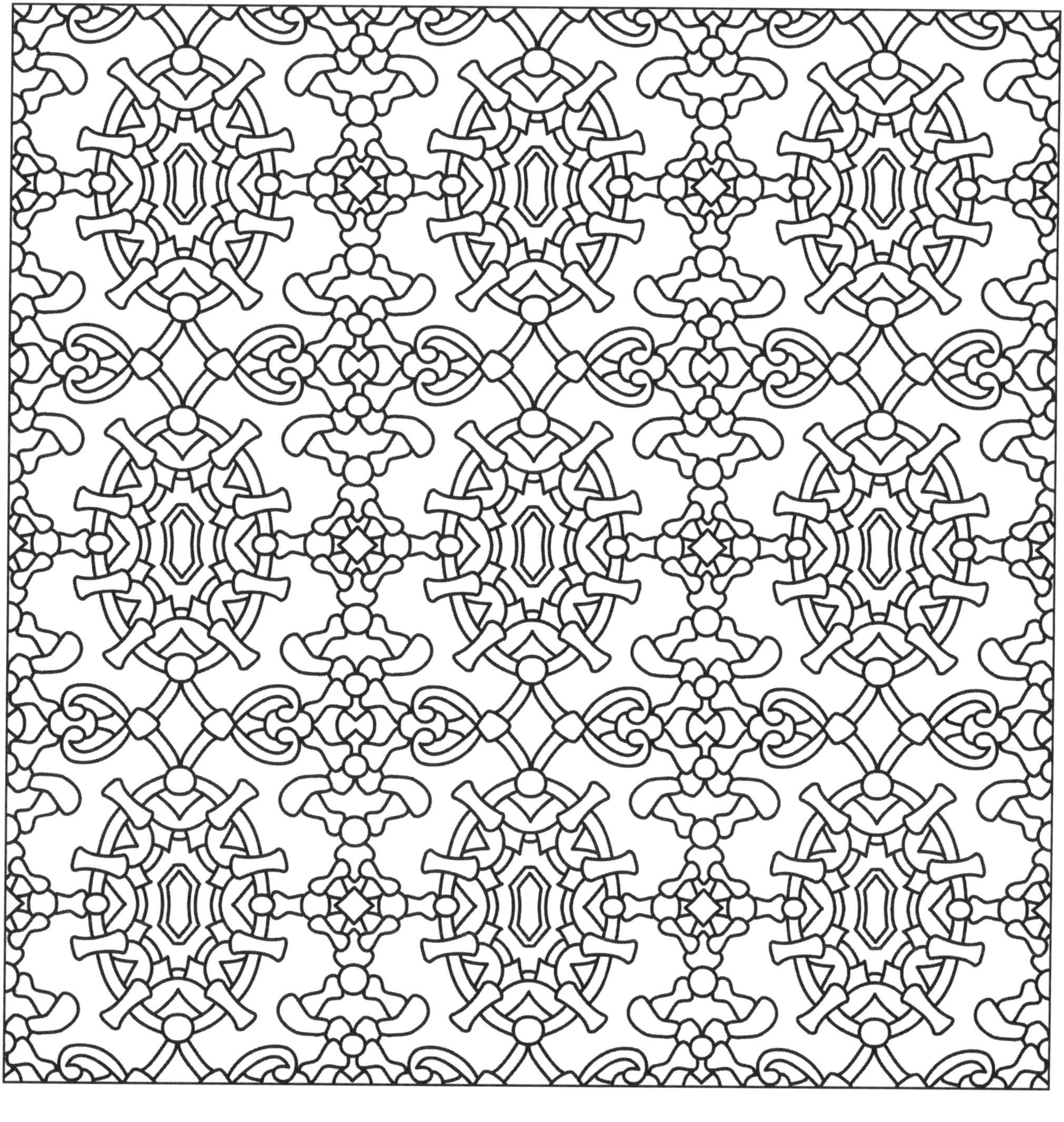

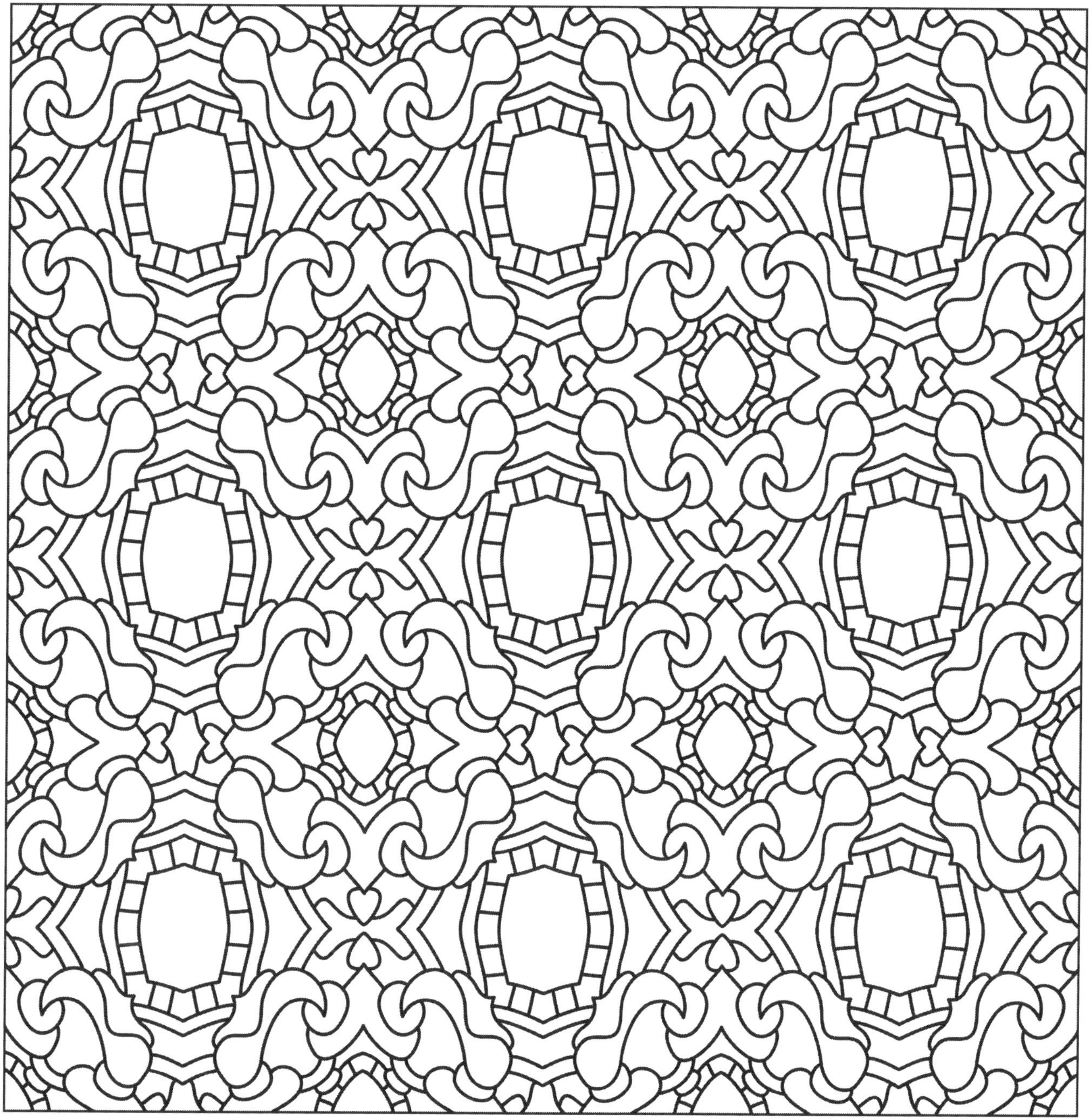

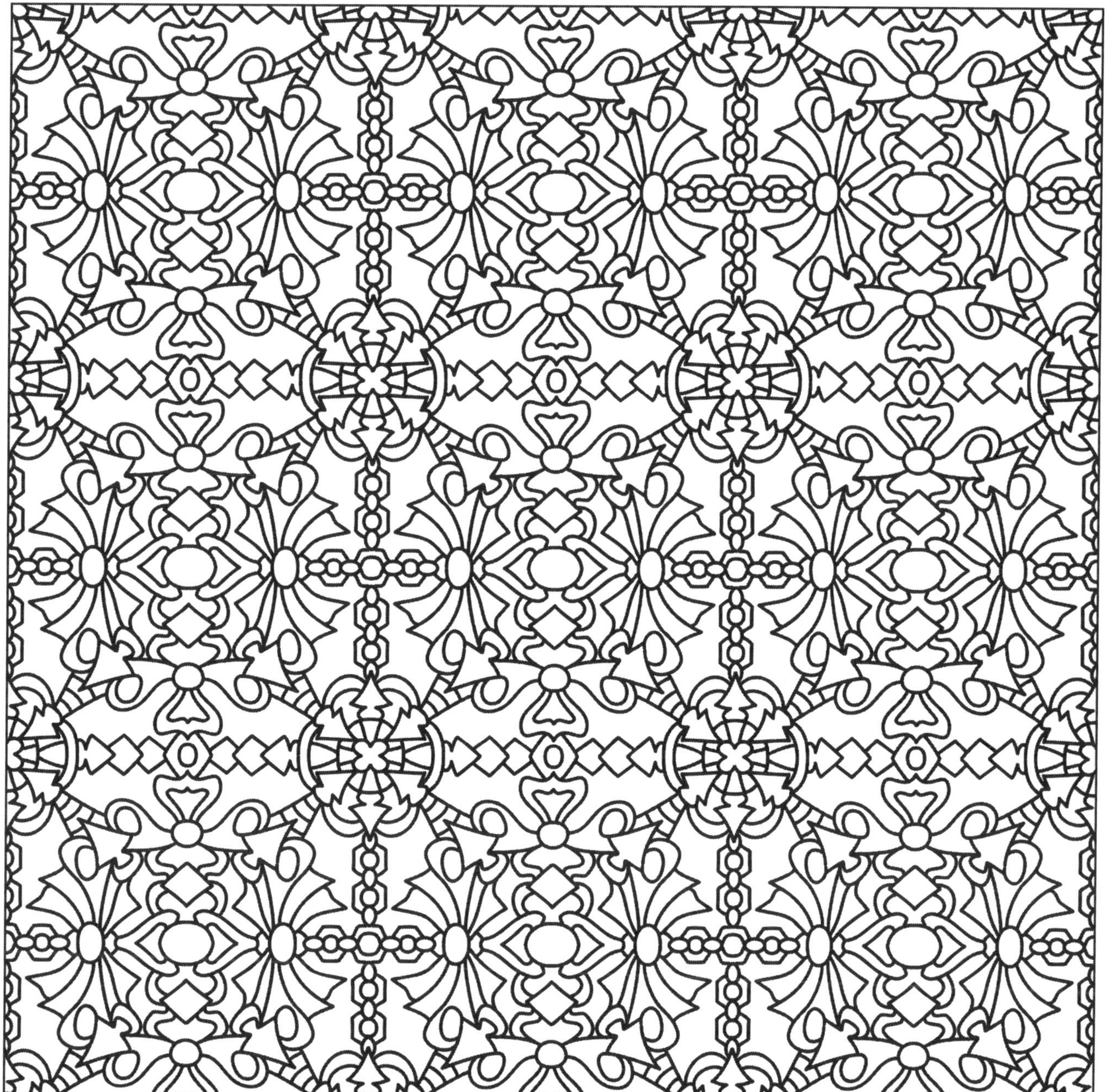

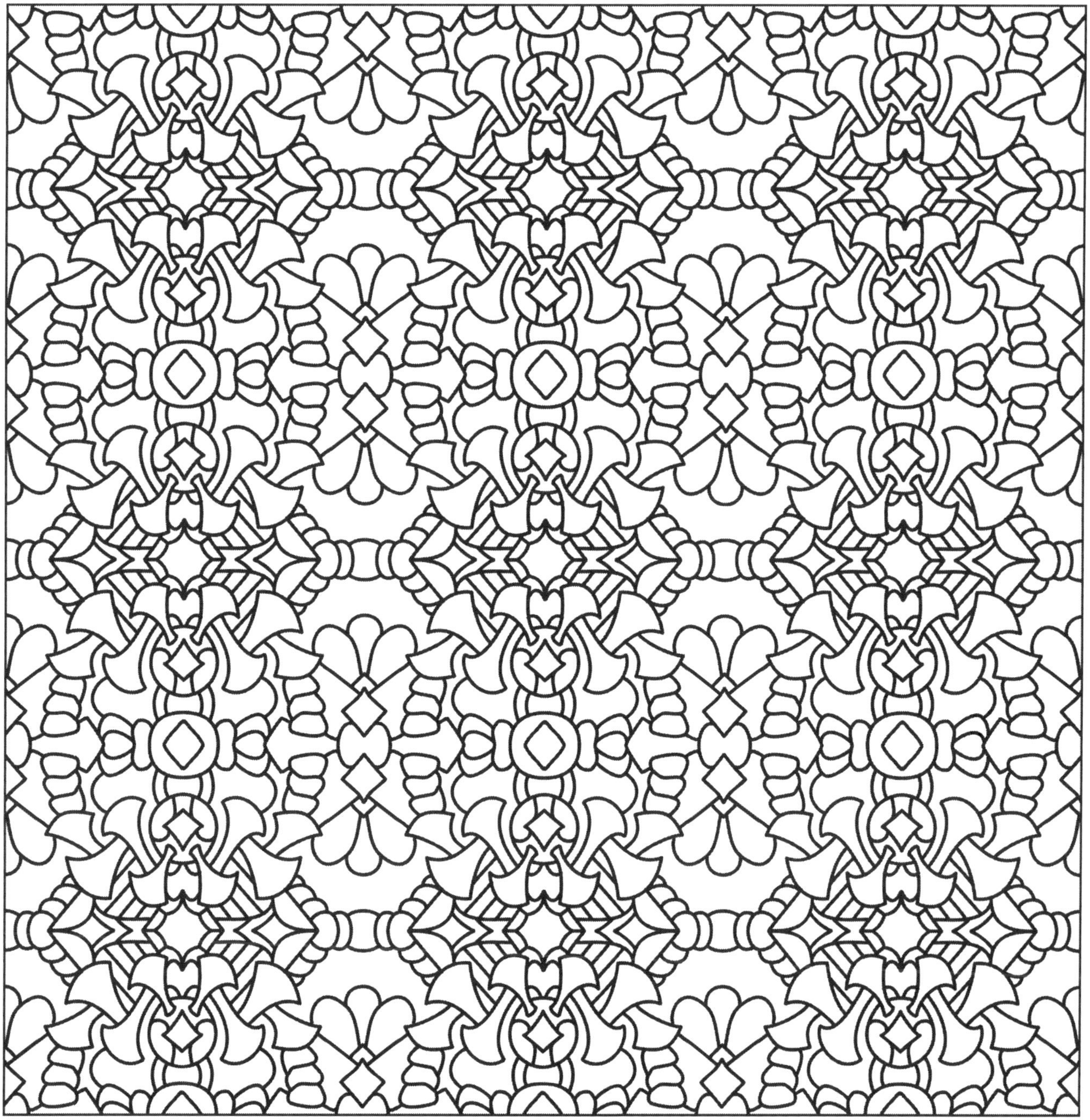

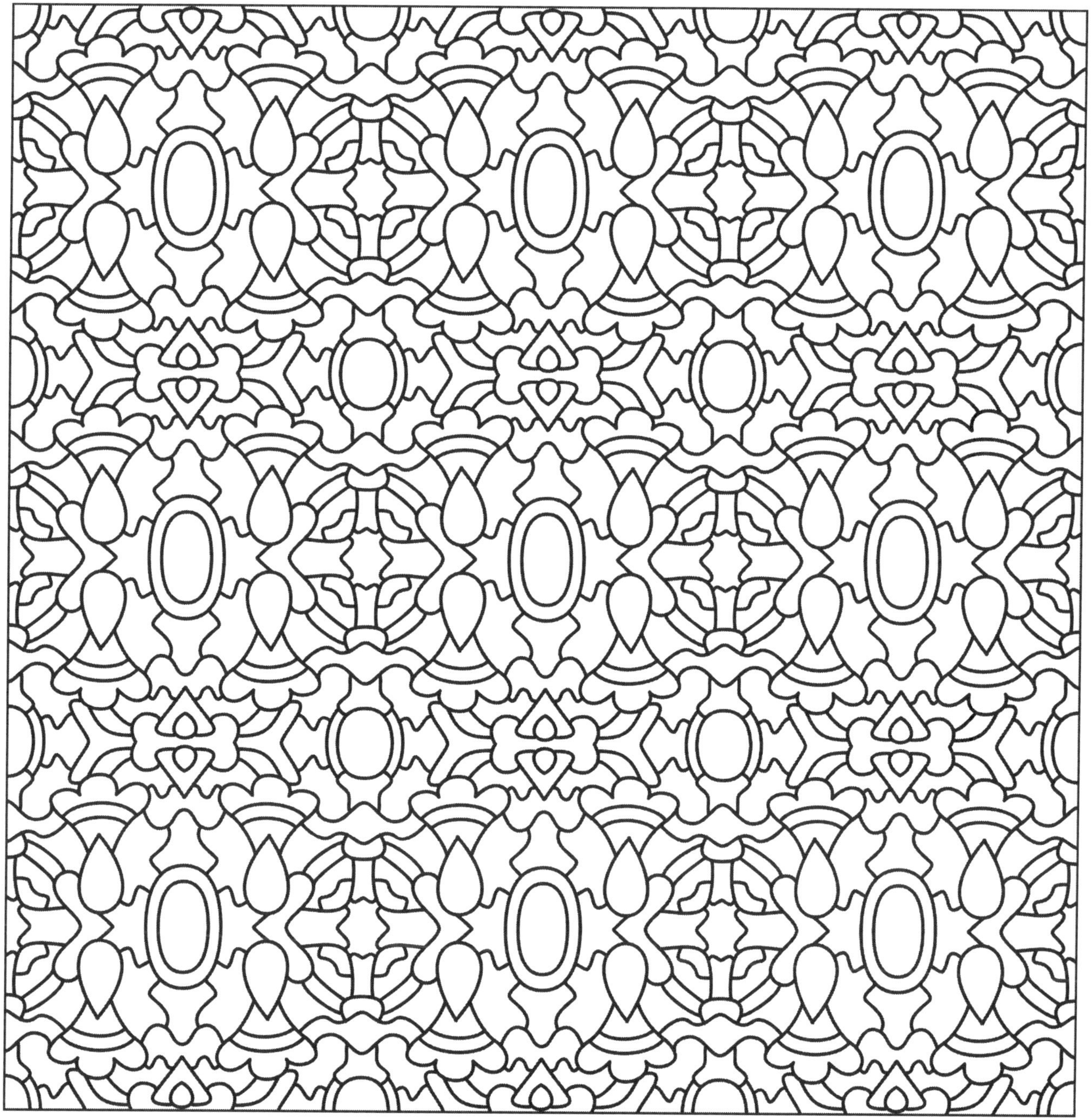

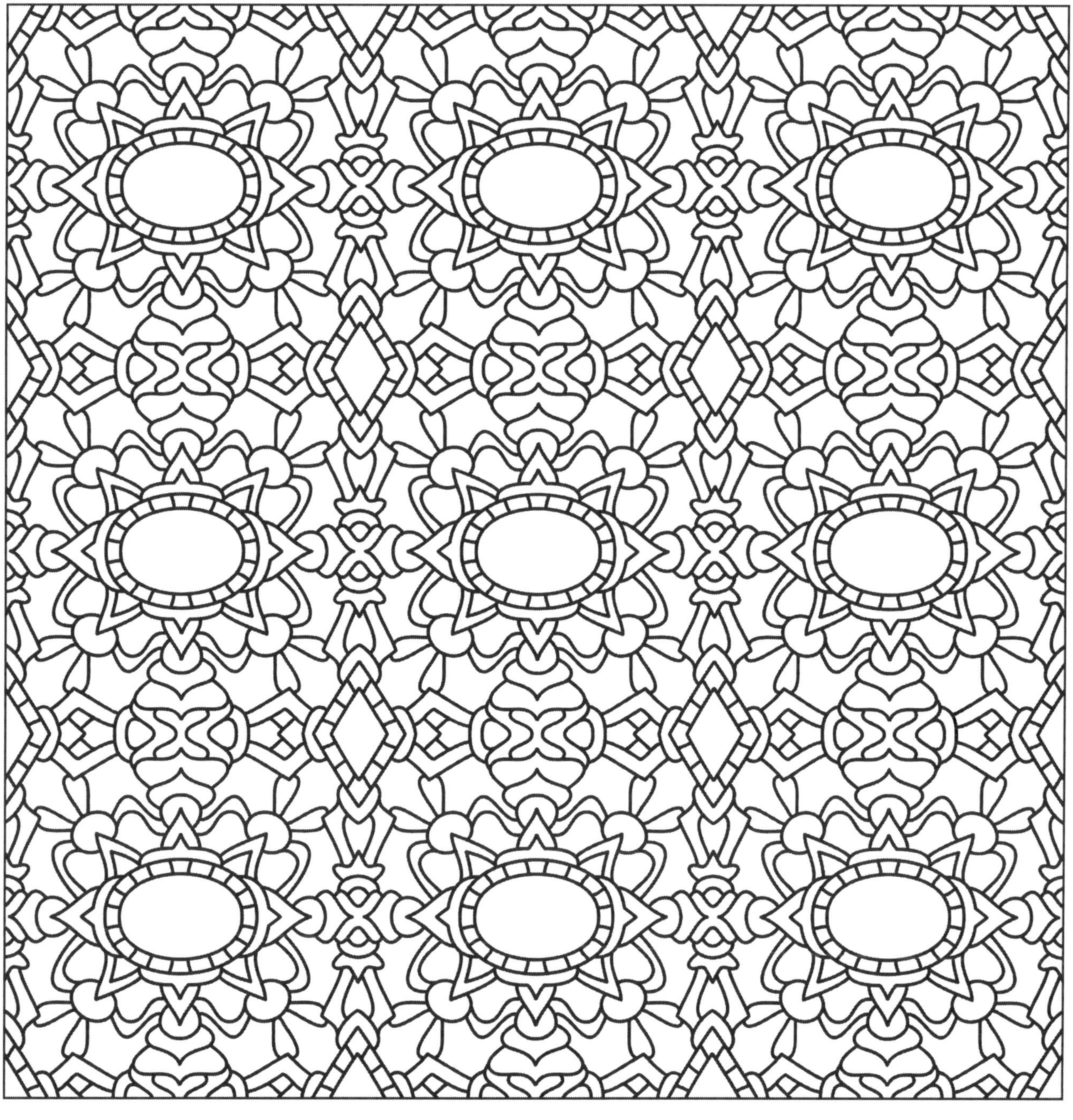

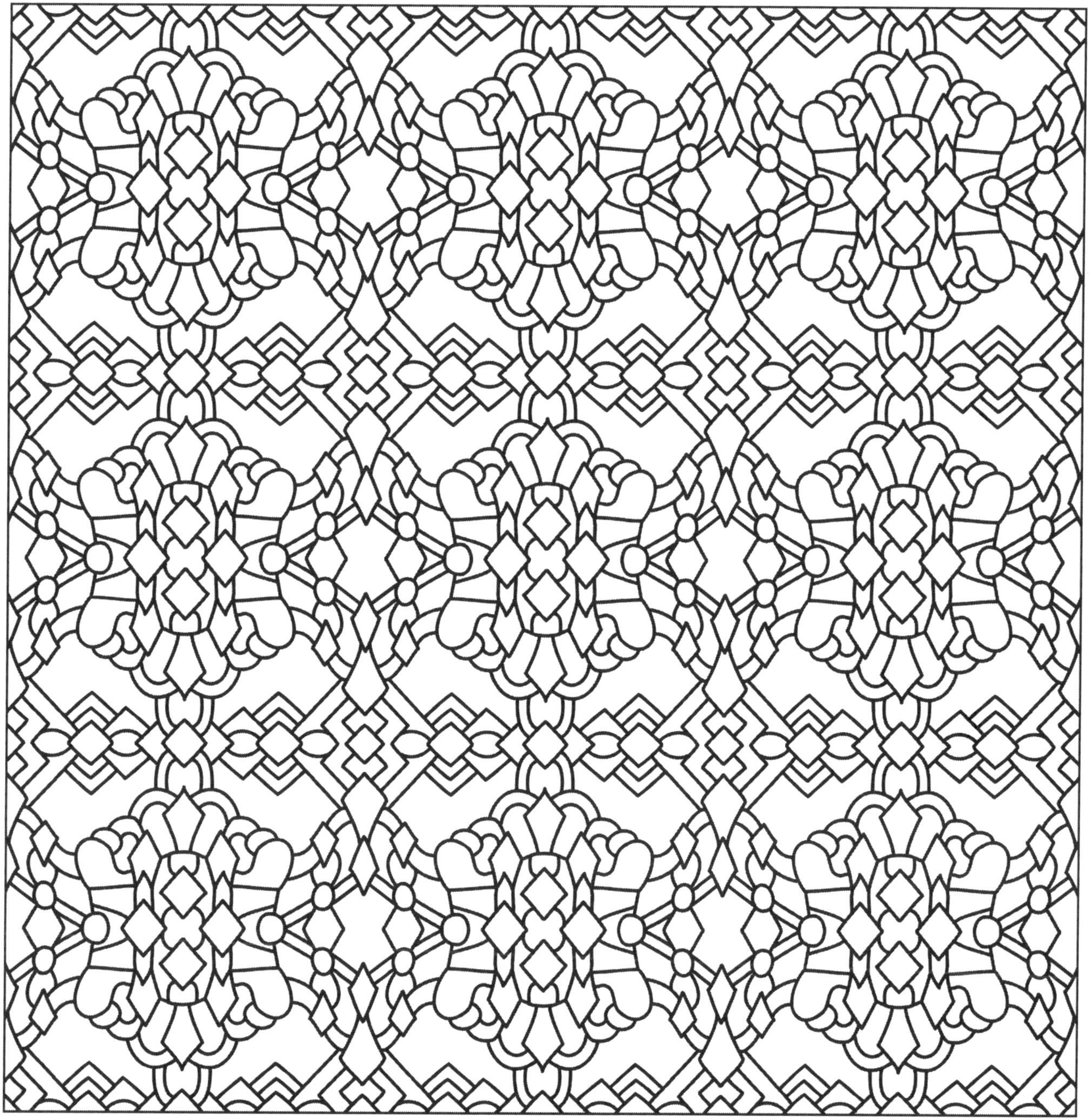

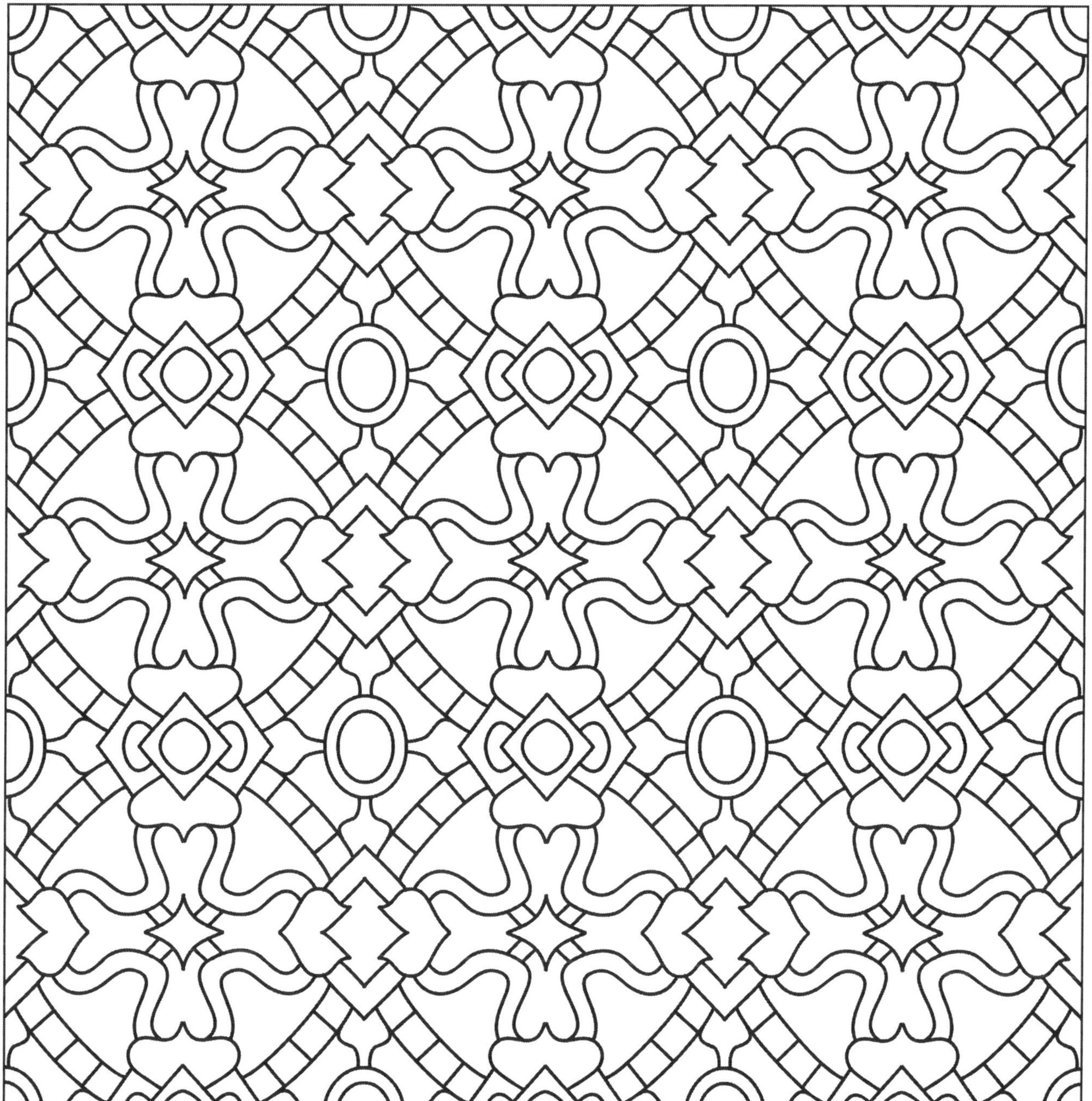

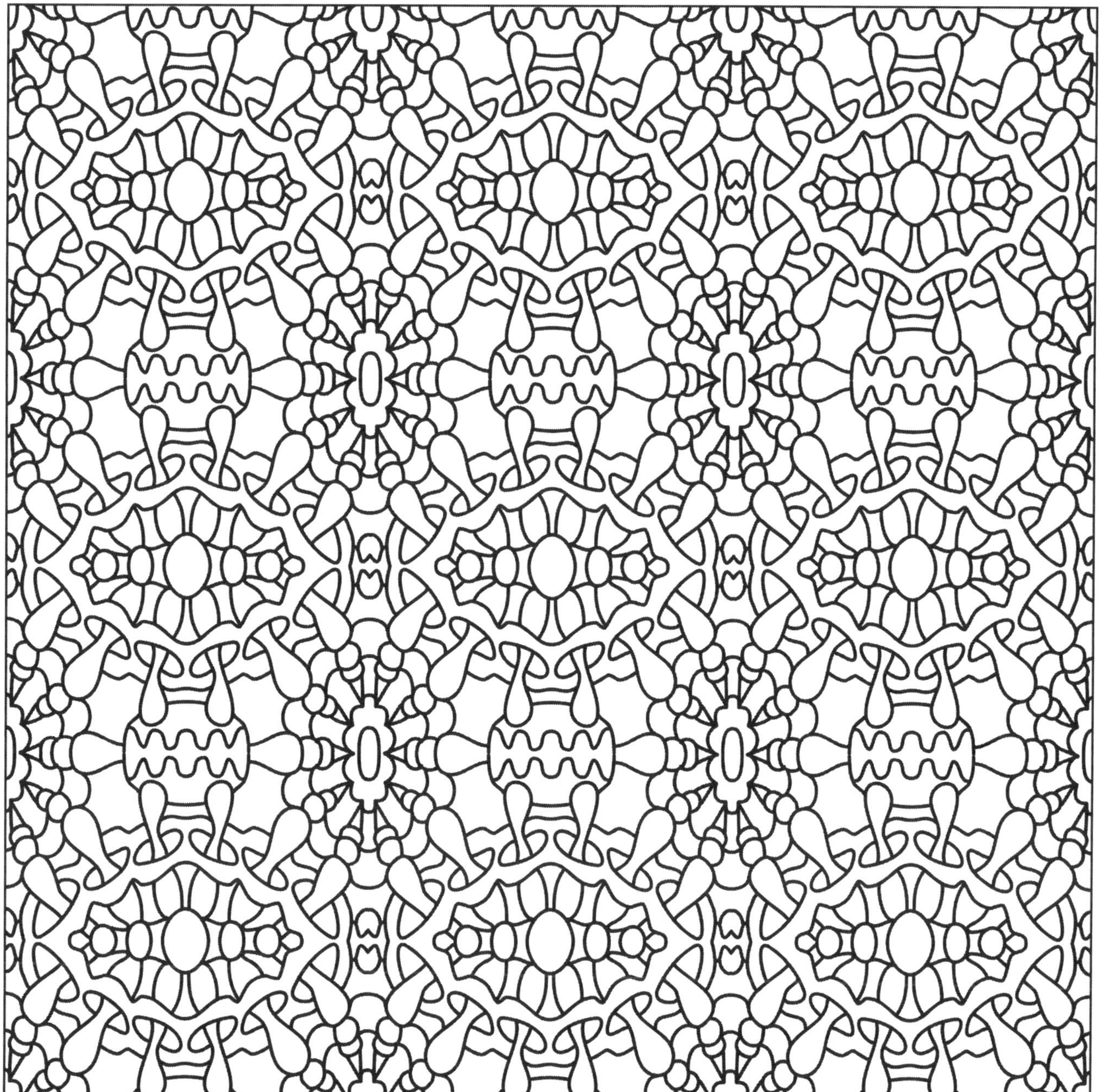

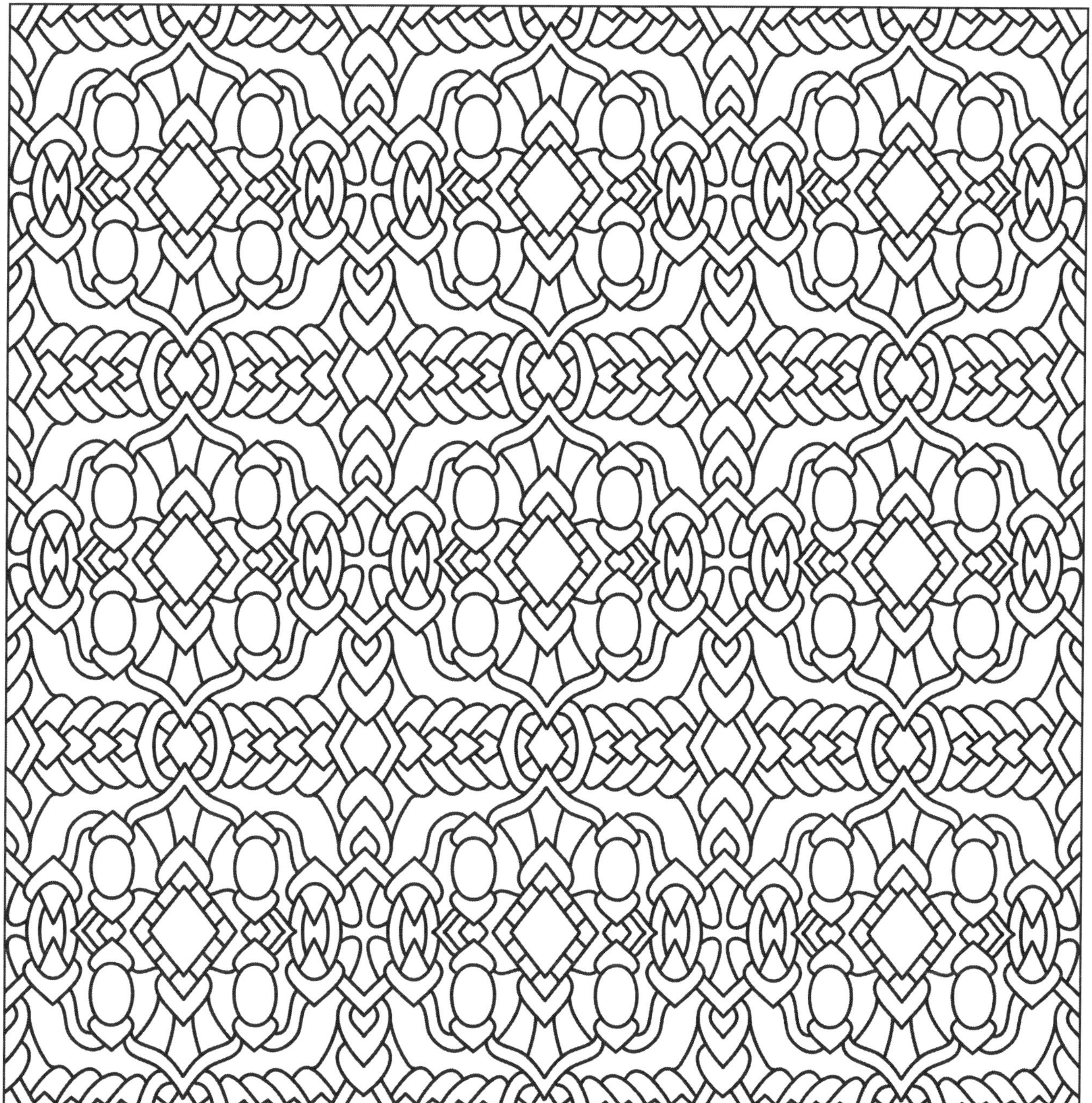

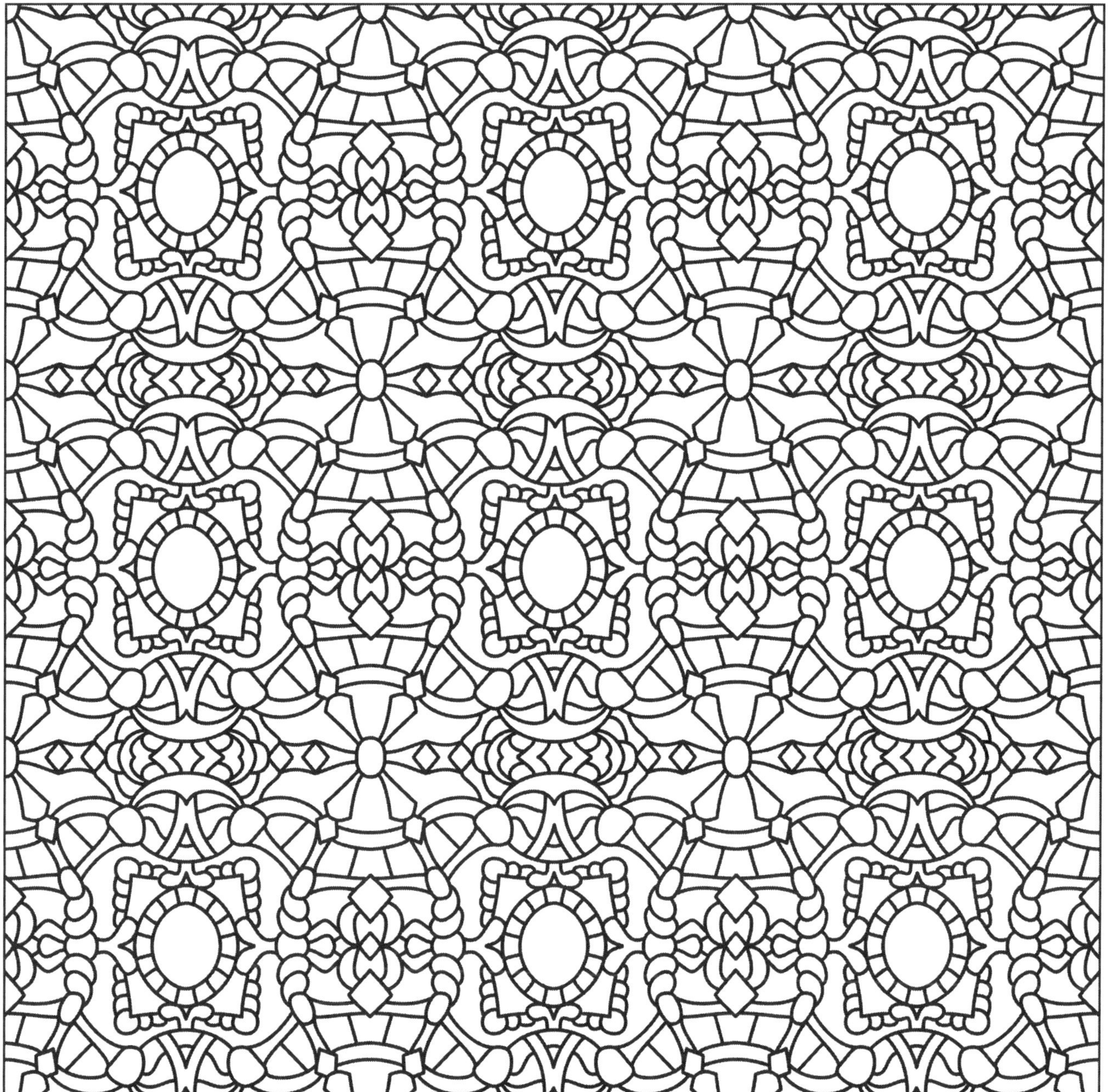

www.AngieGrace.com

Visit Angie's website for special web exclusives.

13025359R00060

Made in the USA
San Bernardino, CA
05 July 2014